On Knowledge and Learning

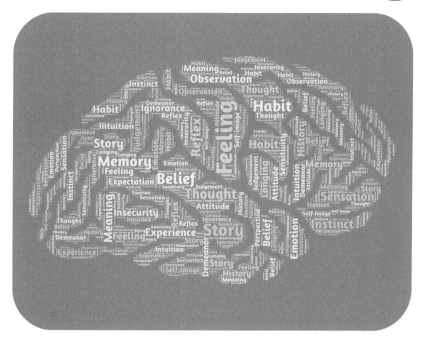

A concise introduction to the humanities

Russell Garofalo
Masahiko Iguchi
Noah McCormack
Patrick Strefford

It is wrong always, everywhere, and for anyone, to believe anything upon insufficient evidence. (W. K. Clifford)

Image credits

Title: Mind Typography from pixabay. https://openclipart.org/detail/223121/mind-typography (CC0 1.0 Universal (CC0 1.0) Public Domain Dedication

World map projections from Wikipedia (Mercator, Hobo-Dyer, Azimuthal: Daniel R. Strebe, Attribution-ShareAlike 3.0 Unported (CC BY-SA 3.0)) 15 August 2011.

The two mysteries: Rene Magritte, 1966, Wikiart public domain.

http://www.trulyfallacious.com/wp-content/uploads/2013/08/equivocation.png

Seven basic emotions: Stu Dunn, from the SDL Behavioral Science Consultancy website

Plutchik's Wheel of Emotions (Wikimedia Machine Elf 1735)

P. 122. Photo by Russell Garofalo.

p. 127. Images by Evan Amos and Anna Langova, Wikimedia.

Chapter 1 The meanings of university education

1-1 What should you study? Why?

To some, the answer to this opening question may seem to be common sense. You should learn deeply about your chosen field of interest. This is so that you can be a more productive member of the workforce after you graduate.

This opening question could also have a deeper meaning, however. If you replace the "you" with "people" as a whole, then the question is asking what people in general should study, and why. Again, the answer may seem to be common sense. People should study useful things deeply, so that they can get good jobs and become more productive workers in the future, and help society become wealthier.

You can see the effects of this view in the real world. Government education ministries, schools and universities all constantly change the contents of the curriculum, as they try to make sure that students learn things that will help them be economically useful or productive. But is the aim of education *just* to help students meet the needs of the economy? Should the economy decide the content and nature of education within a society?

Activity 1.1 The purpose of learning

1. How important is it to you, to learn things that will be "economically useful" at school and in university? Show your position on a scale from 0 (not important at all important) to 10 (very important), and explain your score.

2. What kinds of knowledge and skills do you think will be economically useful in 10 or 20 years time? How certain can you be?

1-1-1 Education for society

Many people disagree strongly with the idea that education systems should focus on economic needs. One practical reason for this is that the economy is changing rapidly and in unpredictable ways. Because of this, it is difficult to know what the economy will be like in the future. Perhaps we only know that the economy in the future will be quite different from today. From this perspective, it seems unwise to use current economic conditions to design education systems.

A somewhat more philosophical reason is that education should meet the needs of society as a whole and not just the economy. So, what does society need? Well, to be sure, there are economic needs that are important. However, surely life is much more than just money. Freedom and independence are also important values, as is participation in democratic decision-making. Individual and group rights may be more important that the economy. Culture, family and the natural environment may also have high value for people. Considering such things, we may say that education should produce active citizens, rather than just productive workers.

In the real world, education is a compromise between many different goals and priorities. All education systems involve practical learning, academic learning, as well as civic education. However, the relative importance of each has varied considerably across both time and space. Importantly, changes in the economy have often been the priority.

1-2 Economic transformation and education

Through human history, technological innovation changed societies and economies relatively slowly. For example, the shift from hunter-gatherer societies to agricultural societies (the Neolithic Revolution), occurred in the Middle East around 10,000 years ago. However, this change took thousands of years to complete. People and societies, therefore, had many generations to adapt to the changes. There was a very slow shift from nomadic life to settled communities. It took a long time to transform from a relatively equal and basic economy to a more complex, unequal and specialized economy. Hunter-gathers tend to work just a few hours a day, all year round, while farmers work harder in different seasons.

1-2-1 Education in agricultural societies

In agricultural societies, most people had no formal education. People learned practical knowledge either from watching others, or by being shown by adults in the communities. Most people worked with their hands. The level of technology was low, change was slow, and the general pace of life was slow. Education did not need to be specialized or systematic. Indeed, people thought that life changed very little over time. People imagined that life for their parents and grandparents had been pretty much the same as it was for them, and assumed life for their own children and grandchildren would also be pretty much the same. In such societies, each community was able to transfer the necessary knowledge to its younger members easily, without formal and intensive education.

1-2-2 The Industrial Revolution

The Industrial Revolution began about 1750 in Britain, spreading quickly to Western Europe and North America. This industrialization was powered by new technologies and fossil fuels like coal, and later oil. Societies that had been rural and agricultural rapidly became urban and industrial. By 1500, about 60% of the population were farmers in Britain, which was the most developed and urbanized country. By 1750, agricultural workers were about half of all workers. By 1900, about 37% of workers were farmers. This means that, over several generations, the society changed from a majority of agricultural workers living in rural areas to a majority of factory workers living in urban areas.

In the US, the Industrial Revolution began in about 1800. However, by 1900, about 40% of workers were still farmers. Thus we could say that it took about 100 years for non-agricultural workers to become the majority. Today, about 2% of the US population is made up of farmers. In Japan, in the Meiji era about 70% of workers were employed in primary industries (farming, fishing, forestry). This dropped to 55% in 1920, and 48.6% in 1950. During the period of rapid economic growth, the percentage went down dramatically to 33% in 1960, 9% in 1985, and around 4% of workers today. Thus Japan's industrial transition, beginning in the Meiji period, also took around a century.

We can see that societies typically had several generations to adapt to huge changes in the nature of work, which typically shifted from farms to factories and offices during the modern era. Importantly, after having lived for thousands of years among relatives and long-term acquaintances in rural communities, people had to adapt to living among strangers in larger towns and cities.

1-2-3 Education in Industrial societies

As people moved to urban areas to work in manufacturing and services, informal education was not enough to prepare them for work. The world was more and more characterized by change, rather than continuity. Because of this, parents and grandparents were not able to teach the young what they needed to know in order to live and work in the new industrial society.

Because of this gap in knowledge, governments introduced mass education systems. Everybody had to learn the same basic skills, including reading, writing, and mathematics. These practical literacy and numeracy skills would help people obtain work and support the modern industrial economy. People also learned national histories and geographies, which combined with the national language created new national identities. These new identities gave people a sense of belonging to a particular nation. This new sense of national belonging replaced the feeling of belonging that people had to the local/rural communities that they left behind. Basically, the government encouraged nationalism so that people would work for industrialization and national development.

Education systems in industrial states also stressed new skills and values that were necessary for the new industrial, urban lifestyle. Schools taught punctuality. Instead of living according to the rhythms of the seasons and the sun, people began to live according to the clocks of railways, schools, and factories. Schools taught self-discipline and obedience, in strict and boring lessons focused on rote learning and memorization. Whereas farmers had mostly chosen when and how hard they worked, these choices were gone in the new economy. People could no longer decide when and how hard they worked. To increase production, factory owners and managers decided that workers had to work long hours of usually dull work. Overall, to make productive factory and office workers, education systems in industrial societies promoted standardization and discipline.

Activity 1.2 Types of learning

Was learning in your school dull and repetitive? Was school education focused on discipline and memorization of facts? How about your personal (non-school) learning experiences (sports, music, jobs, etc.)? Are they the same?

1-3 Economy and society in the contemporary era

Today, in the wealthier industrialized areas of the world, we are seeing a shift towards what is sometimes called a post-industrial or an information society. In these societies manufacturing industries and mass production are less important. Global and information-related economic activity in the service industries are much more important. These include medical, research, law, science, engineering, care work, media, IT, education, leisure and entertainment, fast food, and so on.

1-3-1 Technological change

All of these sectors are being transformed by technological change, which happens very quickly today. Indeed, it seems that technological change is getting faster. Moore's Law says that computer processing speed doubles every 18 months. This rapid increase in processing speed means that technologies spread and new uses are developed quickly. Ray Kurzweil, a famous futurist and key figure in the development of computer technology, says that by 2045, information technologies are likely to be around a billion times more powerful than they are today. If so, in just a few decades, our powers to create and share knowledge will be far greater than now.

A world connected by wireless and wired Internet and personal electronic devices has only really existed for around two decades in the wealthier countries, and around a decade in other regions of the world. During that short time, and relying on these connective technologies, Facebook and Twitter have revolutionized social networking. Airbnb has transformed the rental housing and hotel markets. Services such as Uber are changing the taxi and public transportation industries. Computer algorithms are providing financial and insurance advice, and finding trends in consumer behavior and market trends. 3-D printers are transforming production by allowing people to design and make parts and products themselves without relying on manufacturers. Robots are not only working in factories, but are also beginning to do complex medical surgeries, and do care work for young, old, and sick people. It is amazing to think that these trends have emerged in just the last decade or so. The coming decades are likely to see even faster and deeper change.

Activity 1.3 Jobs at risk

Which jobs seem most likely to disappear, or at least to change massively, because of technological change? How about the opposite, which jobs will continue hardly and change, even with dramatic technological change? Why?

1-3-2 Contemporary trends: from education to learning

Industrialization needs mass-production manufacturing industries, and so education systems followed a similar pattern. Education systems were like factories, mass-producing "standard" workers for the mass-production factories making "standard" goods. However, the creative and information-related industries need much more flexible and diversified education systems. These education systems need to be less hierarchical, less focused on socialization, and more focused on developing a wide range of human abilities. Indeed, in these societies, there is in fact a shift away from education that is merely a one-way flow of information and knowledge from teacher to student. In these societies, there is a shift towards *learning*, which means that people actively and curiously learn for themselves in a more independent way.

Unlike formal school education, learning can take place in many different places, and in many different ways. We could call this informal and flexible learning. This informal and flexible learning, writes the British sociologist Anthony Giddens, may help us in two ways. It may help us to learn practically useful knowledge that helps us to work. It may also help us to become more independent by making us interested in self-development and self-understanding.

1-3-3 Life-long learning

Alongside the shift away from education and towards learning, there is also a tendency for learning to become, more than in the past, a life-long process. Education used to be something that people experience once early in their lives, at school. But, learning is becoming something that must continue throughout life, as we adapt to the technological, economic and social changes.

From this perspective, education should be about developing students' ability to learn, so that the student can deal with an unpredictable future. In this way, the rote learning of facts, such as in the industrial model of education, becomes less important. Contemporary education needs to provide an environment that lets students be creative in their learning, developing skills such as creative problem solving. It needs to train students in high-level critical and logical thinking abilities. These are the key roles of educational institutions that focus on learning for the postindustrial service economy.

Activity 1.4 Knowledge and society

What are the typical everyday tasks in (a) running a farm in an agricultural society, (b) working in a factory or office in an industrial society, (c) doing creative work in a post-industrial society? What skills and knowledge do you need to do them? How can they be taught and acquired? What kinds of changes need to accompany the shift from (a) to (b), and then from (b) to (c)?

1-4 Citizenship and education

Our aim in this course is partly practical, and partly philosophical. Practically, we think that learning to do critical thinking and problem solving is vital in today's connected world, in which we experience a continuous flow of information.

1-4-1 Information overload

200 million people on Twitter are said to send 100 million tweets a day. 35 hours of video content are uploaded to YouTube every minute (equivalent to 176,000 full-length movies a week). Wikipedia has around 4 million articles just in English. Flickr users have uploaded 5 billion pictures. Facebook users have uploaded 50 billion pictures. People send over 247 billion emails every day—mostly spam and viruses, as well as many trillions of text messages a year.

Further, the amount of digital information is expected to increase between now and 2020 by around 44 times.

We live in an overcrowded world, in terms of messages and ideas and content. Parents, teachers, friends, enemies, lovers, advertisers, corporations, politicians, civil society groups, try to influence us. They want us to do what they say, follow their ideas, buy their goods, vote for them, send them money, offer moral support, and so on. Some of them may have good or even great ideas. However, most ideas are likely to be useless, stupid, or even dangerous.

How can we work out what is valuable and what is useless or harmful? Which ideas and people should we listen to? Which ones should we ignore? Which ones should we fight against? Intellectual training in the humanities involves examining arguments and checking evidence. If we can do this, we can independently evaluate the information or idea. This training develops our ability not only to decide what is right (and wrong) and what is true (and false), but also to evaluate information and ideas as "relatively reliable" or "relatively improbable".

Philosophically, we want to encourage you to think about deeper questions. *What can we know? How we can know those things? How sure can we be that our knowledge is reliable?* Learning, researching and discussing these issues will help you to develop critical thinking skills necessary for living a life that is intellectually independent.

To end this introductory chapter, let us propose a different common sense idea: education should result in students learning intellectual skills that will be useful to live in society not just as economic animals, but also and perhaps more importantly, as sovereign political citizens and free social actors. The goal is to empower students in their academic, working, political and social lives.

Memorizing sets of facts or a lot of data is not *that* important. What *is* important is that students learn to examine and understand. Understanding must be the outcome of learning. Students must learn the power of reason. Reason is necessary for any careful evaluation of information and ideas. For example, why do some people believe that education should focus on the needs of the economy? Why do others believe that education should focus on the needs of individuals, or groups in society, rather than the economy? Who benefits and who loses out when what is true is confused with the claims of the powerful?

Until now, your education has probably been focused on learning "facts" about the world. Especially in Japan, but in the Asian region as a whole, university entrance exams tend to be based on multiple-choice questions that require students to choose "correct" information. In most developed countries, university entrance exams require between two to four hours of written examinations involving multiple choice, short paragraph answers, and long essay answers. Indeed, it is thought that essays are really the only way to test a student's knowledge and ability to create something independently.

Whereas written and especially essay answers require that you make statements and give support or evidence for your statements, multiple choice questions do not. They are concerned with your ability to recognize which answer is the correct one. There are no maybes, no gray areas, and no half-truths. Evaluating evidence, judging the relative reliability of different kinds of knowledge, and weighing up conflicting opinions are not something that Japanese university entrance exams values. These are, however, skills that we want you to develop. This textbook has been made for that purpose.

Activity 1.5 Education Styles Revealed in University Entrance Exams

France, Baccalaureate Philosophy exam, 2016. 240 minutes.	*"Why should we study history?"*
Australia, High School Certificate, History exam, 2015. 120 minutes.	*"The past is fixed—no one can change what happened—but as the values of society change, the historians' depiction of the past changes also." Discuss this statement with reference to at least one case study.*
U.K. A-level History 3N Exam 2015 Aspects of International Relations. 90 minutes.	*"The USA's involvement in international affairs in the years 1991 to 2004 was the result of its commitment to the United Nations." Assess the validity of this view.*
U.S. AP History 2015. 195 minutes	*IA) 55 minute multiple choice* *IB) 50 minute short answer a) Briefly explain ONE important similarity in the reasons why new forms of mass culture emerged in the 1920s and in the 1950s in the US.* *II) 90 minute writing* *Evaluate the extent to which increasing integration of the United States into the world economy contributed to maintaining continuity as well as fostering change in United States society from 1945 to the present.*

Japan, Center Exam. 60-80 minutes.	*All questions are multiple-choice. A few brief texts to read as a basis for answering some questions.*

What is required to do well in the different types of exams? What kinds of learning and abilities seem to be emphasized in the different systems?

	Required skills / knowledge
France	
Australia	
United Kingdom	
United States	
Japan	

How do these differences matter? What kind of system do you think is best? Why?

N.M.

Chapter 2 Ways of knowing about the world

2 Introduction

Is nuclear energy safe enough? Can economies keep growing forever, or are there limits to growth? Are shrinking ageing populations really a bad thing? Should states spend lots of money on military defense, or is it better to focus on international cooperation, cultural exchanges, and poverty relief? Are human rights the same for everyone everywhere? Some people might think there are clear answers to these questions. However, it is likely that different people would give very different answers to these questions, and that no consensus exists.

In today's "information society", we have easier access to more data and facts than ever before in human history. However, does all this information help us to understand things more clearly? It seems that sometimes the opposite is true. It may be that it is in fact becoming more difficult to be sure about what is information is reliable, and what is true. It could be that this is a kind of "information overload". It seems that the more we learn, the more difficult it is to be absolutely certain about many things. Reflecting this situation, the Oxford Dictionary Word of 2016 was "post-truth", an adjective describing a situation "in which objective facts are less influential in shaping public opinion than appeals to emotion and personal belief".

Consider the debate on climate change. A 2015 Pew Global Survey indicated that almost three quarters of Latin Americans believe that climate change is a very serious problem. But only 45% of people in the Asia Pacific and 38% of people in the Middle East agree. In the world's two most powerful states, the US and China, 45% and 18% respectively of people think that climate change is a very serious problem.

We have greatly increased our knowledge of climate change science. There are very many scientific experts who now basically agree that climate change is a huge problem. But citizens seem to have very different perspectives. This means that, despite our increased knowledge about the issue, we have not reached agreement/ consensus. People do not agree about what the knowledge means, or whether the knowledge is reliable. This means that action is very difficult.

Table 1 Global opinion on climate change: Pew Research Center (2015)

Regions	Climate change is a very serious problem	Climate change is harming people now	I am very concerned that climate change will affect me personally
Latin America	74	77	63
Africa	61	52	61
Europe	54	60	27
Asia Pacific	45	48	37
Middle East	38	26	27
US	45	41	30
China	18	49	15
Japan	45	71	34

http://www.pewglobal.org/2015/11/05/global-concern-about-climate-change-broad-support-for-limiting-emissions/

1. Why do you think attitudes towards climate change vary so widely? What factors (political, cultural, social, and economic) are likely to influence people's attitudes?

2-1 Common sense as a guide

What is "true" seems to be very different for different people, whether we are talking about climate change, economic policy, or history. How can we know what to trust? How can we know whom to believe? Can we know anything for sure? These questions may not seem too important in your everyday life. You may think that commonsense and textbook knowledge, along with Google and the Internet, is good enough. And yet common sense and general knowledge may not be so safe. They may not be reliable or trustworthy.

Geographical maps tell us what the streets and terrain of the earth are like physically. Common sense is a little like this. It is a kind of mental map that shows us what the world is like more generally. In this way, commonsense tells us things that are true or false, or for things that are right or wrong, reasonable or unreasonable, and so on. Common sense helps us to make decisions in different situations.

Activity 2.2 Mapping our reality

1. Draw a map of the Asia-Pacific region, including 5 political items (cities, countries), 5 geographical features (mountains, rivers, oceans), 5 cultural items (art, music, religion), and 5 arrows showing movement across space (migration, refugees, trade patterns).

2. Alternatively, draw a mental map, with a partner, in which you give some examples of what you think is right / wrong, true / false, good / bad, etc.)

2-2 Intellectual conceptions of the real world

After doing the above activity, we hope that you can understand that mental maps guide us through the various situations of everyday life, just like geographical maps help guide us through the physical world. However, there are problems with both of these kinds of maps. First, lets look at geographical maps.

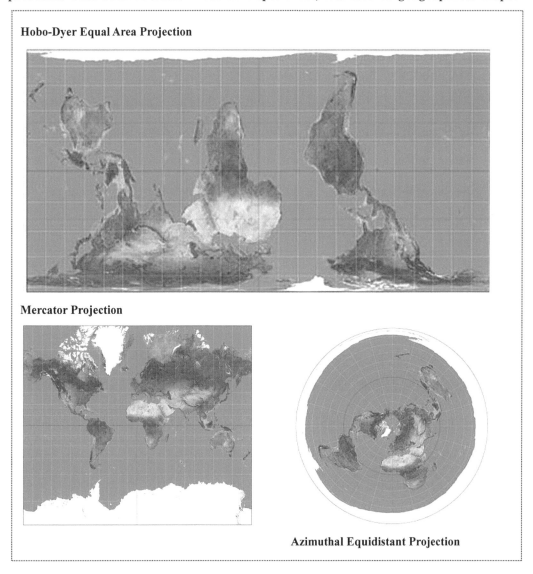

Hobo-Dyer Equal Area Projection

Mercator Projection

Azimuthal Equidistant Projection

The maps below all show the same physical features of the world. But as maps, they are all very different.

Activity 2.3 Mapping the world

1. Are these maps accurate? Why are they so different? What kinds of biases may be involved? Hints: Is the world two-dimensional or flat? Does the world have a top and bottom, or a centre?)

2-2-1 The uses and limits of maps

The Mercator projection makes areas that are far from the equator look bigger. Africa is much bigger than Greenland, but this map makes them look about the same size. It puts north as up and south as down, although 'up' could just as well be outer space, and 'down' could instead be underground. Also, it has Europe at the center!

On the Azimuthal Equidistant Projection, all distances from the center point are correctly represented. However, the distances between them are not right. You may be somewhat accustomed to this projection, since it is used as part of the UN logo, with the North Pole at its centre!

The Hobo-Dyer projection has all the land areas in the right proportions, but the shapes are wrong. Also, the convention of north as up and south as down is reversed, while Africa and South America are at the centre.

Most people probably are familiar with the Mercator projection, and feel that it is normal. People may not be used to the Hobo-Dyer version of the world, and feel it is strange. These feelings are based on what seems normal and right, based on people's experiences in life. But it isn't the case that any one map is correct, and that the others are incorrect. In fact, all maps are incomplete or imperfect. This is logical, if you think about it. A perfect map would have to be the same as the reality it represents. To be perfect it would have to show every tiny detail. It would be too big to be useful Incidentally, the novelist Jorge Luis Borges writes about this problem in his short story entitled "On exactitude in science", in which map-makers, trying to make a perfect map, end up making a map that perfectly reproduces reality 1:1, and so is useless as a map.

In much the same way, our common sense and mental maps are also incomplete and imperfect. Our mental maps are made from our daily experiences. We get information from our family and friends, from books and magazines, from the Internet, from television. Is all this information really 100% safe? Do we check whether all this information is really true? Of course, it is not possible to check all the information we get from all these different places. Thus it is unavoidable that our commonsense contains ideas or beliefs that are not true. It is also very likely that our commonsense has some cultural biases. As with the geographical map, a perfect mental map would have to contain everything, and thus, apart from being impossible, would also be of little use as a map or guide!

Activity 2.4 Maps and territories

1. A well-known slogan says that 'The map is not the territory' (Alfred Kozybski). What do you think this means? What should the relationship between the map and the territory be? How does

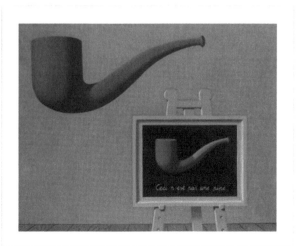

this idea matter to us in this discussion of common sense and mental maps?

2. Rene Magritte's 1966 painting is entitled 'The two mysteries'. The text at the bottom of the painting says in French "Ceci n'est pas une pipe", or This is not a pipe. How is this idea connected to the idea that "the map is not the territory"?

2-2-2 Maps as simplified models of reality

Just as maps cannot be perfect without being the same as the territory that they are supposed to represent, so too mental maps cannot be perfect without being the same as the world itself. Luckily, mental and geographical maps do not have to be perfect. They have to be useful. They are useful if they are similar enough to the real world that we can use them. Therefore, common sense and mental maps can never be a perfectly reliable guide to the real world. This is something that we need to keep in our minds.

Activity 2.5 Global Opinion Diversity: the World Values Survey

Around the world, attitudes towards different issues differ widely. Research an issue from the World Values Survey Wave 6 at the link below, comparing at least five or six countries, and prepare a three-minute presentation about it.

Recommendations: v39 attitudes towards immigrants / foreign workers; v41 people of a different religion; v56 are others fair; v66 fight for country; v81 environment or growth; v127-130 political systems, etc.)

http://www.worldvaluessurvey.org/WVSOnline.jsp

Do you think it is possible to say that there is a correct position on any of these issues?

2-3 Ways of knowing and the problem of uncertainty

It is often said that knowledge is what we are sure is true, while beliefs are things that we think are true, but are not completely sure of. However, the dividing line between them may not be very clear.

A)The sky is blue.

B) Humans are mortal.

C) If a= b and b=c then a=c.

D) It's wrong to kill humans.

Are these statements all true? How do you know? Are they always 100% true for everybody? Perhaps there are many other things that we also think are true, but we are not 100% sure of.

There are said to be eight possible ways of acquiring knowledge about the world: language, reason, perception, intuition, emotion, memory, imagination, and faith. Let us consider each of these in turn.

2-3-1 Language

Language lets humans share knowledge with each other. A lot of what we know is based on what others have told us, or what others have written down for us to read. However, the problem is that you can't always trust what other people say or write. Can you believe cigarette companies or the nuclear power industry when they say that their products are safe? Do other people never misunderstand what you say? Is the meaning of everything that you read completely clear?

2-3-2 Perception

Our senses allow us to see, hear, feel, taste, and smell what the world is like. A lot of what we know is based on the information we get from our senses. However, you can't always trust your senses. Perception happens in the brain, and it sometimes makes mistakes. The brain also has some biases. The Muller-Lyer illusion, and the Shepard Tables illusion, both shown below, are examples of this.

Activity 2.6 Tests of perception

Are the lines the same length?　　　　　　*Are these tables the same size?*

Your answers to these two questions should suggest that our perception is not always reliable!

2-3-3 Reason

Reason, or logic, may seem more certain than other ways of knowing. For example, the example (C) above, "if a =b, and b=c, then a = c" may seem completely certain. But the problem is that most people are not very good at logical reasoning! Let's try!

Activity 2.7 A Test of Reason

A. The number of false statements here is one.

B. The number of false statements here is two.

C. The number of false statements here is three.

D. The number of false statements here is four.

Which statement is true? (There is one true statement)

2-3-4 Intuition

Sometimes, you may feel that you know something just because it seems obvious. But just because something seems obvious to you doesn't mean that it is true. It is also a little risky to assume that what is obvious to you is also obvious to someone else.

Consider this: During World War II, many American soldiers were conscripted into the army. Some were from the city, and some were from the countryside. Which group—city or countryside—do you think found it easier to deal with the difficult living conditions of an army at war? Was your intuition correct?[1]

2-3-5 Memory

We can know about the past based on our memories. All of what we know is, in a sense, based on memory. If we lose our memories, then we lose all of what we know. But memories are not perfectly reliable. Details can change or be forgotten, while it is even possible to gain memories of events that never happened! Indeed, we remake memories each time we remember them. A simple Google search for "false memories" will provide you with many examples of this!

2-3-6 Emotion

Our emotions, such as fear, disgust, happiness, and sadness, affect how

---

[1] A famous 1949 study by Paul Lazarsfeld, based on surveys with 600,000 US soldiers, found that urban background soldiers tended to be much happier with military life than rural background soldiers. Does this match your sense of what is intuitively obvious?

we perceive the world. Some events and people are frightening, while others are stressful. Some people are a joy to be with, and others are not. But while emotions can be a useful way to know about the world, strong emotions can also be harmful to knowledge. For example, we are more likely to believe things said by people we like. In the same way, we are less likely to believe things said by people we dislike. Deep sadness can make everything look negative, while joyful love can have the opposite effect. In this way we can see that emotions are a problematic way to get knowledge.

2-3-7 Imagination

Imagination is perhaps a surprising way of knowing. But we use it all the time. For example, you are walking through the forest, and you find that a bridge over a river has collapsed. You look at the river, and you have to think, can you jump across, or should you go back, or look for another way across. To decide whether you can jump across or not, you need to use your imagination: Have you jumped that far in the past? Is it likely that you can jump that far now? You could know these things directly by jumping! But it is better if you use your imagination first, to try and work out if it is safe enough to jump. Obviously, sometimes your imagination is going to be wrong, and you may get wet or experience various kinds of failures. (Even in failure, or course, you will have learned something!)

2-3-8 Faith

To have faith in something is to be committed to believing in it, even without proof, in an unquestioning way. You might imagine that faith is typically religious, but it is equally common in romantic or corporate relationships. Religious faith involves unquestioning belief in core elements of a religion, such as the claim that Christ is the son of God, or that karma exists, without having much proof. Romantic faith could involve believing that you and a partner are committed to each other, again, without solid proof. An example of corporate faith is when teammates on a sports team or soldiers in the same unit or workers in the same company unquestioningly believe that they will look out for and support each other.

Some key points about faith are that it is not necessarily based on proof or fact, and that it is accepted without question. Whether faith is justified is a problem, however. Another issue is that some people's faiths are likely to contradict those of others, and this leads to conflict.

2-4 Knowledge as doubtful

None of the ways of knowing seems to offer 100% definite knowledge. If so, then can we actually be absolutely certain that anything is true? Can we be 100% sure that we even exist in the world? Thinking, said Descartes, is proof that we exist. But this doesn't seem very satisfactory. Although it is highly unlikely, it is not absolutely impossible that we are dreaming that we exist as thinking feeling humans on earth.

2-4-1 Relativism

Because nothing seems to be absolutely certain, some people may feel attracted to a philosophical idea called relativism. Relativism says that no absolute objective truth exists. Relativists think that truth is relative and subjective. This means that something can be true for an individual or a group at a particular time and place. But for another individual or group, that thing might be false. Everything depends on the person or the group. Truth is relative to the situation of each person or group. This means that we cannot say there are definite truths for all of humanity all of the time.

However, can we seriously agree with the idea that true and false, good and bad are relative things? If some people think global warming isn't happening and others believe it is, are both positions equally valid? Can something be happening and not happening at once? If parents don't believe in Santa Claus, and children do, are both beliefs equally valid? Can someone exist and not exist at the same time?

The relativist idea that there is no universal and absolute truth seems hard to accept. It must be that some people's beliefs are wrong (assuming the world is not a contradictory and multiple place!). Relativism actually depends on one absolute truth, that "all truth is relative". Paradoxically, to believe in this truth, however, would mean that you are not a true relativist. As a theoretical position, relativism is difficult to justify.

Activity 2.8 On Moral Relativism

Consider the following three scenarios. For each, fill in the blank with morally "obligatory", "permissible" or "forbidden."

1. A runaway train is about to run over five people walking on the tracks. A railroad worker is standing next to a switch that can turn the train onto a sidetrack, killing one person, but allowing the five to survive. Flipping the switch is _____.

2. You pass by a small child drowning in a shallow pond and you are the only one around. If you pick up the child, she will survive and your pants will be ruined. Picking up the child is _____.

3. Five people have just been rushed into a hospital in critical care, each requiring an organ to survive. There is not enough time to request organs from outside the hospital. There is, however, a healthy person in the hospital's waiting room. If the surgeon takes this person's organs, he will die but the five in critical care will

survive. Taking the healthy person's organs is _____ .

Is the answer to all of these obvious? Would you accept that different answers are

as valid as your own?

From Marc Hauser and Peter Singer (2005), "Morality without religion".

2-4-2 Balanced judgment

After this discussion, it may seem that deciding what to believe is quite difficult. You may think it is difficult to judge what is true and what is not. On the one hand, we need evidence and we need to be skeptical. But, on the other hand, we should also keep an open mind.

To take a religious example, a global survey of religiosity and atheism by Win-Gallup in 2012 among more than 50,000 people in 57 countries found that almost 60% of the world's population believes in a religion (14% and 16% in China and Japan respectively), whereas only 13% believe there is no god (47% and 31% in China and Japan respectively). The atheists should try to keep an open mind about the possibility that there is a god or some gods. This means, even though there is no real evidence, it is possible that believers are right. On the other hand, the believers should try to keep in mind the lack of evidence for the existence of god. They should be skeptical about what they believe, and keep their minds open to the possibility that the atheists are right.

Overall, we should try to carefully consider the available evidence. Based on this evidence, we can make conclusions, but we should be ready to change our conclusions if the evidence changes. In other words, we need to find a balance between being skeptical and having an open mind. This will help us to work out what knowledge is reasonable, and what knowledge is unreasonable.

Activity 2.9 Testing for ESP

Do you believe in ESP (Extra-Sensory Perception)? Do you believe it is impossible? Well, we can do a kind of test for telepathy, which is a form of ESP, using a simple testing kit containing five cards, each with a different image on it: a circle, a plus, wavy lines, a square, and a star, as well as a data collection sheet. We will need groups of four: an experimenter, a subject, and two observers. The experimenter will go through cards and send mental images of each one to the subject, with the observers watching. The subject will try to say what the card is, with the observers noting down both the actual card and the subject's response. Later, we will calculate the percentage of right answers. But before we begin, what percentage of correct answers would you consider to indicate that telepathy occurred? (If you just guessed, the rate should be around 20%, but how high would the rate need to be, to be a sign of ESP?)

Procedure

The experimenter shuffles the cards, and then goes through them in order, making sure that the subject cannot see them. The experimenter will try to send a mental image of each card to the subject. The observers will record what the image on the card is, and the response of the subject. The third column is to record the result: a circle for a hit, and a cross for a miss. After each member in the group has had a turn as subject, we will collate the results, and calculate the percentage of hits and misses.

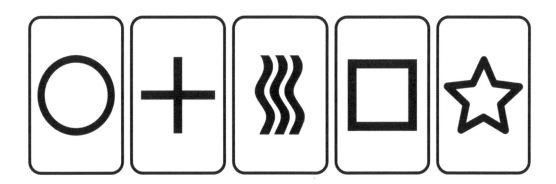

2-4-3 Reasonable knowledge

If some knowledge is based on evidence, and if it is a good fit with other knowledge that we are relatively sure about, then it is probably reasonable. These two conditions, evidence and coherence with what we already know, are very important in deciding whether a belief is reasonable or not.

If someone claims to be an alien, you'd hopefully want some positive evidence, such as a DNA analysis showing that they have non-human genes, to prove it. The argument that you can't prove they are not an alien is not a good reason to believe them, since not being able to disprove something is not proof that it is true.

If someone claims to be telepathic, again, we hopefully would like to see positive proof, and lots of it, in order to believe them. Again, the argument that we cannot prove someone is not telepathic is insufficient to be proof that they are. Such claims are called arguments from ignorance, and they mistakenly assume either that a) because something has not been proved false, it must be true, or b) because something has not been proved true, it must be false.

Activity 2.10 Reasonable and unreasonable conclusions

Add another sentence to these phrases, to turn them into arguments from ignorance, following the model given in the example.

Example: X is in love with you, I'm sure. I haven't heard anything that suggests otherwise.

1. *No one has put forward any proof that UFOs exist. Therefore...*

2. *Scientists can't prove that global warming is occurring. Thus...*

3. *There's no proof that Joe committed the crime. So...*

4. *There's no proof that you're a terrorist. Consequently...*

Next, suggest some reasonable additions to the first sentence.

2-4-4 Confirmation bias

Another issue concerns the human tendency to focus on evidence that supports what they believe, and to ignore evidence that goes against what they believe. If you believe artists are creative and engineers are not, for example, you're likely to find examples of creative artists and uncreative engineers. At the same time, you're likely to overlook examples of creativity in engineers, and lack of creativity in artists. This tendency is known as confirmation bias. Because of it, it is important to look for evidence against our own beliefs as well for proof of what we believe. In this way, it is important to test our beliefs.

As well as looking for sufficient positive evidence for our beliefs, we should also consider whether our beliefs are a good fit with other beliefs that are considered reasonable. This is called *coherence*, and it is necessary because, despite the importance of being skeptical, we can't be skeptical about everything. Being skeptical doesn't mean that we have to doubt absolutely everything. We need to start with some assumptions about what is currently understood to be reliably true.

At the same time, being open-minded doesn't mean we have to be open to all possibilities equally. Beliefs that are not coherent with what we understand to be true, which go against current knowledge, need more evidence for us to believe them. For example, ESP such as telepathy or mindreading goes against what is commonly believed about human mental abilities. To accept ESP as truth, we would need very strong evidence.

Activity 2.11 Coherence in everyday life

1. *One day, a "good" student submits work of excellent quality. Another "bad" student also submits work of excellent quality. How will the teacher react? Why?*

2. *Is it more likely that ghosts exist, or that aliens exist? Why?*

2-5 Conclusion: Does it matter what we believe?

Are some beliefs better than others? Should we care whether or not our own beliefs are really true? Should people be free to believe whatever they like?

Our common sense comes from our experiences in life. We learn it from the people and situations that we experience. Unfortunately, many common sense beliefs are likely to be unreliable or even mistaken. If you don't want to go through life believing in things that are not true, then it is necessary to use critical thinking about what you believe.

Further, what we believe affects what we do. For people who don't believe in global warming, there is no need to do anything about it. For those who believe that human life begins at conception, abortion can never be justified. Religious people who believe that their religion is the only true religion, and that all unbelievers will go to hell, may find killing or oppressing unbelievers to be right. Nationalists who believe their own country is superior to all other countries may believe that aggressive military action against others is right or just. Men who believe in the inferiority of women will avoid hiring them for higher-level positions. Members of Japan's Zaitokukai believe that non-Japanese, and especially Resident Koreans, should be killed, or at least expelled from Japan. Some people may believe, because alcohol and cigarettes are legal, that they are safe drugs, and use them.

These examples, ranging from everyday life to international politics, suggest that what we believe matters, both to individuals, and to the societies that we live in. Critically thinking about the things we believe and why we believe them, is necessary for us to live our own lives as subjective human beings. It is also necessary for us to be good citizens of a global human society.

Activity 2.12 On the Beliefs of Others

1. Should we respect the beliefs of racists, sexists, and other kinds of fundamentalists?

2. Give some examples of what you think are mistaken and dangerous beliefs.

3. Do you think it matters, if other people have what you think are mistaken beliefs? Does anyone have an obligation or a responsibility to change those people's minds?

N.M.

Chapter 3 The Nature of Knowledge

3-1 Introduction: knowledge as justified true belief

What is knowledge? Can we answer this question easily? The answer is no, we cannot answer the question easily, and the reason is that knowledge is a *thick concept*. We must think deeply about it in order to understand it. In contrast to this, examples of thin concepts are good or bad. In this chapter we will investigate and gain a deeper understanding of knowledge. We will begin by looking at knowledge defined as justified true belief, and then we will look at some different types of knowledge.

3-1-1 Truth

The difference between knowledge and belief is truth. If you know something, you must think it is true. However, if you believe something, then you just want it to be true. For example, someone may *believe* that aliens live on earth, but they do not *know* it. Given the absence of evidence, they can't *know* it is true, however much they want to *believe* it is true. We must be very careful about this difference.

If we look at the history of thought, then we can see that in the past people believed that the earth was flat, or that the earth was the center of our solar system. In the past, people believed these things to be true, so for them, at that time, it was knowledge. However, we now know that the earth is not flat, and that the sun is at the center of our solar system. We can see that knowledge changes over time. This is as it should be. Humans are curious animals, always trying to learn new things, and so it is natural and desirable that knowledge expands over time. This means that in the future, there will likely be new pieces of knowledge, and some of our existing knowledge may turn out to be false (can you think of any examples?).

So, this brings us to the important question of how can we be sure that the knowledge we have really is true? Well, as we know from previous chapters, we can never really be 100% certain. The standard we use is 'beyond reasonable doubt'. 'Reasonable Doubt' is a concept used in the criminal justice system of many countries. In court the prosecution must use proof, or evidence, to show that the person is guilty of the crime. This proof or evidence must be strong enough that a reasonable person has almost no doubt that the person is guilty. Of course, we did not actually see the crime, we are not 100% sure that the person really did commit the crime, but the prosecutors must try to convince impartial reasonable observers that the person did it. So, just as in the law, when we say our knowledge is true, we really mean it is true 'beyond reasonable doubt'.

3-1-2 Belief

Belief is when a person thinks something may be true, whether or not they have proof, or evidence that it is really true. As we said in the last section, we can say that if a person believes something, they want it to be true. If someone believes something, we could say that it is their opinion, or their attitude. Importantly though, it does not mean that it is true. We do not need to think deeply to believe something. For example, before we go to bed at night, we don't think deeply about whether or not the sun will rise the next morning. We assume that it will. In this way, beliefs are often based on assumptions that we do not check. This is why many people believe things that are not true!

It seems obvious, but to know something is true, you must also believe it is true. In this way, belief is necessary for knowledge. We cannot say we *know* something, if we do not *believe* it. Because of this, we cannot say that a map knows where Germany is, or that a plane knows where Kansai International Airport is. How about robots? Can we say a robot has knowledge?

The relationship between knowledge, truth and belief can be shown in this diagram, where the overlap between truth and belief is knowledge. However, it is not so simple!

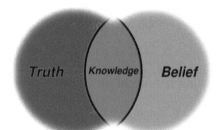

Instead, we should use what is called a belief-knowledge continuum, as shown below. On this belief-knowledge continuum, knowledge is at one end (the right side), and unjustified beliefs are at the other end (the left side). These unjustified beliefs are highly unlikely to be true. Here we can see that knowledge is +10 certain, or very close to that. As we have said before, it is very difficult to be 100% certain, so we use the "beyond reasonable doubt" idea that was previously discussed. To the left of this, we have +5 probable, which we call well-supported beliefs. We are not as sure about these beliefs as we are about our knowledge, but we have spent some time thinking about these beliefs. We have checked: we have done some research. But, we need to think more and do more research if we want to call these beliefs knowledge. Then, to the left, we have vague beliefs. These are beliefs that perhaps we heard somewhere, or we read somewhere, but we are really not sure about them. We wouldn't want to take action based on these vague beliefs; it would be a little dangerous! Let's have a look at some examples.

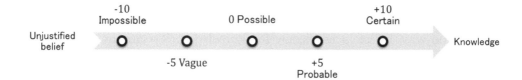

Perhaps your mother told you when you were small that if you eat too much chocolate your nose will bleed. Perhaps you believe this now. But are you sure? Is this really knowledge? Have you thought deeply about this, and done some research? If someone asks you, can you explain clearly and in detail why eating too much chocolate makes your nose bleed? If you can, then we can call it knowledge. We can say that you know eating too much chocolate makes your nose bleed. However, if you cannot, then we must call it a belief. But, which type of belief is it? If you have thought about why chocolate makes your nose bleed, if you have done some research, and discussed it with someone, then perhaps we can call it a *well-supported belief.* However, if you just remember that your mother said it to you when you were ten years old, and you have not thought about it since then, we must call it a *vague belief.*

We have many vague beliefs. These are things we have heard or read somewhere, but we don't really think about them normally. Perhaps we could say that these vague beliefs are not really necessary. If they were necessary things then we would think more deeply about them and change them into knowledge, or at least well-supported beliefs.

So, what is an example of a well-supported belief? When you have some proof or evidence that suggests something is probably true, but you are not confident enough to say that you know it is true. For example, you are watching a murder/mystery drama on TV, and you have seen lots of evidence indicating that

Mr. Plank was the murderer. But the drama is not finished yet, and even though you think that Mr. Plank is probably guilty, you don't want to say you *know it*. While watching the drama, we have been listening carefully to what the detective says, we have thought carefully about the proof or evidence that has been shown. Because of this process, we can say it is well-supported belief. But, still we didn't actually see Mr. Plank kill the victim.

Finally, a belief that is *beyond reasonable doubt* is knowledge. We know that the Holocaust happened during World War Two. Even though we were not there and did not actually witness, or see, the events, there is so much evidence that it is very difficult to say it did not happen. We have seen dreadful photos and film of the concentration camps, we have read many stories written by survivors, and countless books have been written about the Holocaust. It is reasonable to say that we *know* the Holocaust happened.

Activity 3.1 The belief-knowledge continuum

Put the following things on the belief-knowledge continuum. Then add a few of your own. Make sure you can explain your decisions.

1. *Aliens have visited earth.*

2. *The rise of China is a threat to Japan.*

3. *God(s) exist(s).*

4. *Singapore is on the Equator.*

5. *The universe is infinite.*

6. *Japan is dependent on the US.*

7. *If X is longer than Y and Y is longer than Z, then X is longer than Z.*

8. *Murder is wrong.*

3-1-3 Justified

So far, we have said that knowledge must be both true and believed. In this way, knowledge is that area where truth and belief overlap. However, there is one more important part of knowledge. As we have discussed, true beliefs, or knowledge must be based on evidence, which means we must have justifications. Furthermore, knowledge must be justified in the right way. What does this mean? For example, there is lots of evidence to say that astrology cannot be used to make predictions about the future. I also do not usually believe in astrology. However, imagine one day, I read my horoscope and believe one of the predictions. Now, imagine that this prediction actually comes true. Did I know it was right? It seems irrational. I had no evidence. It was surely just luck, or chance. Is this really knowledge? Well, obviously it is not. Knowledge must be justified in the right way. So, how do we justify our knowledge?

To justify our knowledge we must use the ways of knowing that we have already looked at. We can use language, perception, reason, intuition, emotion, memory, imagination or faith as justifications for our knowledge. Let's look at some examples.

- *"I know something because someone told me".* Where can you put this on the belief-knowledge continuum? How about, *"I know something because my mother told me",* and *"I know something because my younger brother told me"?* Would you put these two in the same place on the belief-knowledge continuum? Obviously, some people are more trustworthy than others, which means that things that they tell you are more reliable than things that other people tell you. Different people have knowledge about different things. If a professional footballer told us something about football, then probably that is a reliable source, but how about if that same professional footballer told us something about the best camera to buy? Is that knowledge as well justified? Different people have knowledge about different things. Needless to say, we usually check things that people tell us. This means that if we think something that is told to us is important, then we should check that information in another way.

- *"I know something because I saw it"*. Where can we put this on the belief-knowledge continuum? How about, you are standing in the corridor outside the classroom and you just saw your teacher go into the classroom. *"I know my teacher is in the classroom because I saw her go in"?* Can we be sure that this is justified in the right way? Perhaps. But, maybe the teacher left the classroom by another door. Or it might have been someone dressed up to look like your teacher. How about another example? You witness a crime and the criminal runs past you. You see his face clearly, but only for an instant. Then the police catch the criminal and put him in a lineup, which includes 5 or 6 other men, who all look similar. It's a little bit strange, but imagine that the police tell you that if you correctly identify the criminal, he will go to jail. There will be no trial, just you as a witness. Are you sure enough to send the criminal to jail? How about if the crime is murder, and the police tell you that if you correctly identify the criminal, he will be hanged. Again there will be no trial, only you as a witness. Are you sure enough?

- We can also use the other ways of knowing that we have already discussed. For example, *"I know something because I worked it out"*. This is reason, which is perhaps the safest way of knowing. Or, *"I know something because it's obvious"* (intuition), or *"I know something because it feels right"* (emotion). Alternatively, *"I know something because I remember it"* (memory), *"I know something because I can empathize"* (imagination), or *"I know something because I have faith"* (faith).

3-1-4 Justification and responsibility

We should say that some of these ways of knowing are more reliable than others. The more reliable ways of knowing are better ways to justify our knowledge.

Importantly too, if you say that you know something, in a way, you are responsible for that. Imagine that someone asks you directions on how to get to the train station. If you give incorrect information, then that person could get lost. You have to be responsible in your answer. Imagine another situation, in which someone asks you if it's safe to swim in a river near your house. You must be responsible in using your knowledge to answer the question.

3-2 Levels of Knowledge

So, we have looked into knowledge a little bit more deeply and discovered that it is best to say that knowledge is justified true belief. Now we must look again at knowledge. This time, lets look at the different levels of knowledge. We could divide knowledge into the following three levels: shallow knowledge, which is a superficial understanding of something; deep knowledge, which a good understanding of something; and expert knowledge, which is complete mastery of something. Of course, there is another level: ignorance, or no knowledge, which is a complete lack of understanding about something.

Let's look at some examples. A small child may know that his mother is a teacher, but his level of knowledge about this is obviously totally different to his mother's. Similarly, a professor's level of knowledge in their specialist subject area is obviously very different to that of a student of the same subject area. As you study a subject in depth, your level of knowledge will deepen over time.

It may be that much of the knowledge we have is merely shallow knowledge, meaning that we have only a superficial understanding. At school maybe we studied weather patterns and weather formation, but do we now have a good understanding of the weather in the area in which we live, or do we just check the weather forecast to see if it will rain today?

It might also be that much of what we think we know is just second-hand knowledge that we have picked up from somewhere. As we previously said, we should double-check our knowledge, but it may be that we often don't do this. In this way, much of our knowledge may be shallow knowledge. For example, is remembering something for a test really knowledge? Much of the education in schools is focused on studying to pass exams. These exams are often multiple-choice questions (A, B, C, D, etc.), and so students need to just remember some facts. Is this knowledge? Does this lead to understanding? We will look at this a little more shortly.

It is interesting to consider whether we understand more of the world around us today, in the 21st century, than our ancestors did, say 10,000 years ago. Of course, due to scientific breakthroughs we now understand about plate tectonics, gravity, electricity or DNA, but we also use many appliances and other technology of which we may understand very little. How much do we really understand about the great scientific breakthroughs that are so necessary for our modern life? How much do we really understand about the cool gadgets we use every day? In this way, can we really say that our understanding, or our level of knowledge about the world in which we live is really much greater than our ancestors who live so long ago?

Much of our knowledge may be only little bits of information that we have collected, and this brings us to our next topic.

3-3 Knowledge and Information

It is important for us to understand the difference between knowledge and information. Imagine a three-year old child who can count from one to ten. Does that child really understand the numbers? Can that child really count? Can that child count and collect ten balls if told to do so? Well, possibly the child could, but possibly not. Small children copy parents and older children without understanding what it is they are doing. Young children can also memorize the words to songs. Indeed, this is an important way for them to learn language. But, when they first copy, they possibly do not understand what the words mean, or what the song is about. When the child first copies the words to the song, they are merely repeating, "parrot-style".

As we discussed before, remembering pieces of information for a test does not necessarily lead to knowledge. What is the difference then, between information and knowledge? Well, knowledge is much more than just lots of pieces of information. Knowledge involves understanding how different pieces of information are connected. It involves understanding causal relationships, or how something causes another thing to happen. If we look at the figure below, called the DIKW pyramid, we can see how information and knowledge are different. Data is at the bottom. Data is merely numbers. However, this data is necessary for information. Indeed, we could say that information is built with data. In the same way, knowledge is built with information. Or to put this another way, information is necessary for knowledge. The same can be said of wisdom at the top.

We could also say that each level is made up of the bricks for building the next level. So, pieces of information are the bricks that we use to build knowledge. The bricks must be connected, or put together, to make the building. Only when the bricks (information) are put together, can they make the building (knowledge).

There is one more final point to make here about the difference between information and knowledge. While we can pass on pieces of information, while we can read a book, or discuss something with our friends, we can only make knowledge in our own brains. Even if our professor tells us something, even if we study something in depth in class, we must put that new information into our brains and connect it to the knowledge we have there already. This is another important way in which we must be responsible for our knowledge. We cannot just download knowledge. We must build it in our brains. This is especially true in university where we are building academic knowledge.

3-4 Types of Knowledge

There are different ways to separate knowledge into different types. There are different ways because people disagree about the different types of knowledge. We should also say that people disagree about what is, and what is not, knowledge. It's important to remember that these types of knowledge are not totally separate and unconnected types of knowledge. The different types of knowledge we will introduce are all connected. When we categorize things into different types, it is to try and simplify so that we can understand. It is the same with these types of knowledge. What follows is perhaps the simplest way to look at types of knowledge.

Knowledge of something

We can call this knowledge by acquaintance, which is first-hand knowledge, based on perceptual experience. For example, you have knowledge of your hometown because you live or lived there.

Knowledge how to do something

This is practical knowledge that comes from having a skill to so something. For example, you may know how to ride a bicycle, or how to speak a foreign language.

Knowledge that something is

This is knowledge by description, which is second-hand knowledge. When we read something, or when we are told something, this is knowledge by description. Most of the knowledge that you build up through your studies at university is this type of knowledge by description. This is academic knowledge. We will investigate this academic knowledge at another time.

For now, we will look at the first two types of knowledge, which we can both call *experiential knowledge*.

3-4-1 Knowledge by Acquaintance

First-hand knowledge is perhaps the most basic way in which we know things. As babies, we get knowledge this way. Babies get to know the world around them by touching, tasting, smelling, etc. The first words that young children learn are the words for those things that are around them. Indeed, for young children this is really the only way to learn, to know. Children must experience things in order to learn. The best way to teach a child that fire is hot is to slowly bring their hand closer to the fire so that they can feel the heat. The child is then learning first-hand that fire is hot. Perhaps adults are the same in some way. We often say that, no matter how much you read about the beauty of some place, "you really have to go there". For example, we have seen many photos of earth from space, we have seen many movies about astronauts, we know what zero gravity means, but only someone who has been into space really knows what it is like. Only someone who has had that experience, is acquainted personally with that situation and that environment, really knows what it is like to be in space. Other people can only imagine, and even though some people are very good at imagining, it is not the same as actually experiencing something.

It is perhaps useful to think about people when we try to understand the difference between knowledge as acquaintance and knowledge as description. We can describe our family or friends, but really it is necessary to actually meet someone in order to know them. In our modern world, we get lots of information about famous people, but can we really say, "we know them", just from the things we read about in the newspaper? Perhaps we can say, "we know something about them", but this is really a different thing. Or perhaps we should say it is a different level. We have a deep level of knowledge about our family and close friends. We are very well acquainted with them. We have lots of experience of doing things with them. There are other people that we know very little about. Perhaps we have met them only once or twice. In this case, we have only a superficial, or limited knowledge about them, because we have limited experience of interacting with them.

We should say, however, that while first-hand experience is an essential source of knowledge, there are some limits. Sometimes, for example, we cannot explain, in words, what we have experienced first-hand. Can you explain what coffee tastes like? Or chocolate? Can you explain what it is like to climb Mount Fuji in the darkness, see the most beautiful sunrise you have ever seen from the top, and look down on the Alps through the clouds below? Sometimes we say, "you have to see it for yourself".

It is also true, unfortunately, that our memories fade over time. This means that we forget lots of the details of the experiences we have. Importantly too, we now know that our brains remake memories each time we remember them, and this means that memories can change over time. If this it true, then there is a danger that the knowledge we got from an experience is lost over time, or worse, that the knowledge changes over time. Is this still knowledge?

Activity 3.2 Memories and experiences

1. What is the nicest memory you have of when you were at elementary school? Explain in as much detail as possible to your partner.

2. Explain the following experiences to your partner.

A. The taste of natto.   *B. The smell of fresh bread.*

C. The taste of lemon juice.   *D. Being blind.*

3-4-2 Practical Knowledge

It is important that we remember that knowledge is not just *knowledge of the head*, but also *knowledge of the hand*. Knowledge of the head means that descriptive knowledge that we learn in formal education, or read in books. Know-how, or knowledge of the hand is all that practical knowledge that we have. It may be that we have some collective bias against knowledge of the hand, and in favor of knowledge of the head. In Japan, for example, people tend to think that university education is of a higher standard than education in vocational school or *senmon gakko*. In fact university graduates also get a higher salary than graduates from vocational schools. Vocational schools in Japan are often of a very high standard. The students have to study very hard. It seems that sometimes university students in Japan don't study so hard. Should we still think that knowledge of the head is somehow better than knowledge of the hand?

It may be that this prejudice comes from the idea that human's ability to think logically and rationally is what separates us from other animals. However, our opposable thumbs also separate us from most other animals. The opposable thumb allows human to use tools. We should say of course, that a number of apes also have opposable thumbs, as do giant pandas. In this way, animals too have practical knowledge.

As young children, we spend a lot of time getting practical knowledge. We learn how to crawl, then how to walk and run. We learn how to use pencils and chopsticks. We learn how to talk and ride a bicycle. This is all practical knowledge, know-how. Even when we go to school, we continue to get new practical knowledge. Indeed, we should say that this textbook too is full of know-how. Of course, we first study in a textbook, and this is descriptive knowledge, but this knowledge should also be practical. You should be able to apply this knowledge to your life. This knowledge should give you new skills that you can use. This textbook has many exercises where students have to apply, or use, what they have learned in a real-life situation. This is practical knowledge.

Many times, it is necessary to practice something for it to become knowledge. Learning a musical instrument is like this, as it sport, or language. This is why a textbook like this has practice questions.

Activity 3.3 Practical knowledge

1. *Make a list of the different kinds of practical knowledge you have. What new practical knowledge have you gained recently?*

2. *What practical knowledge do you want to get in the future?*

3. *Should schools focus more on practical knowledge, and less on descriptive knowledge?*

3-4-3 Explaining know-how

Can we explain how to do all the practical knowledge that we have? Probably we think the answer is yes, but let's see... Can you simply explain how to do something simple? For example, can you write a simple explanation for how to tie your shoelaces? Or, how about, how to use chopsticks? Have you ever tried to read an instruction booklet for a new appliance, and not been able to understand what to do? Lego famously have instruction booklets that have no words at all. Of course, it could be that making a Lego toy is relatively simple, and so words are not necessary.

Being able to explain how to do something may be a good test of our practical knowledge. Certainly, good teachers are able to explain difficult things, so that students can understand them.

Activity 3.4 Explanation exercise

1. *Choose one of the following and explain how to do it in the simplest possible way. Use as few words as possible.*

   A. *How to tie a shoelace*   B. *How to use chopsticks*

   C. *How to wash your hair*   D. *How to write the alphabet (ABC)*

3-5 Conclusion

We began this chapter with a discussion of knowledge as justified true belief. We looked at the difference between truth and belief, and the relationship to knowledge. We then used a continuum to show the different levels of belief. This showed how some things we believe are really just vague beliefs that we are not so sure about. We then discussed how to justify our beliefs so that they are not false. We considered the different ways of knowing that we have already studied.

We looked at the different levels of knowledge, from superficial knowledge, through good understanding to expert knowledge. Then we looked at the difference between knowledge and information, and we learnt that information is, in some way, the building blocks of knowledge. Importantly too, we learnt that knowledge can only be built by us, in our own brains.

We then looked at different types of knowledge focusing on knowledge by acquaintance and practical knowledge. These both form personal knowledge that we will talk about later.

P.S.

Chapter 4- Language

4 Introduction

Language is one of the Ways of Knowing. Can you remember the other Ways of Knowing? Take a moment and try to remember them.

To begin with, what is language?

When we talk about language, normally we mean the languages used by humans to communicate with each other, like Japanese, English, and French. These are formal languages that have their own sound system and writing system. They are spoken, heard, read, and written.

Actually, though, in its broadest sense, language is any method used to communicate. It can be done using any of the five senses: sight, sound, smell, taste, or touch. Humans have highly developed language systems, but if we consider language simply to be a method of communication, then many animals also have language.

For our study, however, we will focus mainly on human language and what it includes. A more technical definition of language is that it is a highly developed information storage and transmission system that involves using symbols, images, letters, gestures, sounds, and objects.

Some languages have no writing system; they are oral languages only. The many languages of Aboriginal people in Australia are an example. Although Aboriginal languages do use pictures to communicate meaning, they have no developed writing system such as the Roman alphabet (for Romance languages), or pictograms (for the Chinese language).

Activity 4.1 Language characteristics

1. Name as many languages as you can.

2. Which languages use an alphabet?

3. Which languages use symbols or pictograms?

4. Does your language have a writing system? Explain the writing system of your language.

5. Which languages are only oral?

6. Are there any languages that are only written, or only typed?

4-1 The importance of language

Language is such an important part of being human that all humans living with others learn a language automatically, without even trying. There are many books that claim to help children learn their native language at younger and younger ages, but these books unfairly target new parents who are worried whether or not their children are developing at a normal rate. The truth is, whether parents try to teach their native language to their children or not, the child will learn that language. Only in the very rarest of cases, just a couple of known cases in the history of the human race, has a child grown up without learning a language, and that is because that child was kept away from any spoken human interaction during the first years of her life. These are rare cases of abuse and hardship. Otherwise, a child, by nature, will learn a language. It is impossible not to learn one.

In fact, some scientists and linguists believe that the human brain is specifically structured for language learning. The great thinker Noam Chomsky said that children have an innate sense of grammar. Indeed, our brains seem to be structured specifically for acquiring language. To explain further, the brain is composed of millions of brain cells, called neurons. Research has suggested that some neurons have the specific job of processing the meaning of verbs, while other neurons help us process the meaning of nouns, and still others the meaning of adjectives. This suggests our brains are made for language. Maybe this is why it is so easy for children to learn a language.

Although, it is also true that some aspects of language are time sensitive. That is, research suggests that if a child hasn't been exposed to the sounds of a particular language by a certain age, that child will never be able to speak that language with perfect native pronunciation. A child will lose the ability to detect and thus pronounce particular sounds in the Danish language, for instance, if it hasn't heard it by the age of one year.

Activity 4.2 Language and sounds

1. Which sounds in English are easy for you to say? Which sounds in English are hard for you to say? Why do you think this is so?

2. Which sounds in your language do you think are hard for foreigners to learn and say? Why do you think this is so?

3. Do you agree with the research that suggests that our brains are specifically made for language learning? Why or why not? (If you doubt this fact, try doing a little research and find out in what ways our brains are specifically structured for language learning.)

4-2 Language and ideas – what comes first?

You have probably heard the familiar question, "What came first, the chicken or the egg?" It is a philosophical question and a scientific question that is very hard to answer. Once you start arguing for one side, the chicken, you realize that you could equally be arguing for the other side, the egg. (Of course, the correct answer is to say that the question is misleading: neither chickens nor eggs suddenly appeared. Life evolved slowly over time, with chickens being distant descendents of egg-laying dinosaurs!)

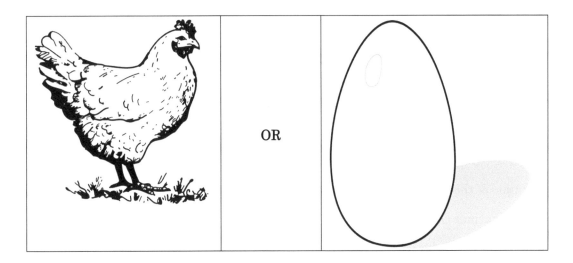

Likewise, with language, it is hard to say if language reflects the ideas we already have inside us, or if language forms the ideas we have. Which comes first, the language or the idea? Again, it seems like the only practical answer is both came from some prior condition or circumstance.

If you have ever observed a baby, you'll notice that a baby has a lot that it wants to express. It wants food. It wants drink. It wants that toy on the other side of the room. It wants to have its diaper changed. Clearly, these are things that the baby wants or needs independent of language. Some toys it finds scary. Some toys are boring. Some toys it really loves. The question is, is the baby thinking these things, or do these ideas only exist after the baby has learned the words and what the words mean?

4-2-1 Concepts before words

Let's take one side of the argument first. We could argue that a baby can only learn words if it has the related idea already in its mind. In other words, a baby can't learn to say, "This game is boring" until it is a few years old. But even from the time before a baby can speak, it has the feeling of boredom. It doesn't know the word 'boredom', but it has the feeling that equals boredom. Thus, it learns this word that just fits into the idea of boredom that already exists in the baby's mind. The idea comes first.

4-2-2 Words before concepts

Now let's look at the other side of this argument. There is the often-used example of the Inuit people who have many more words for snow than people who live in warmer climates. One might say, in this case, that the idea only exists after one has learned the words. That may be true, but in any case, everyone who has seen snow can identify snow, whether they have a word for it or not. It is part of the natural world and picked up by the senses. Again the idea is there first, or in this case the natural phenomenon. However, the degrees to which one can identify it may indeed be the product of language, a pure idea.

In this way, it could be said that sometimes language comes first, sometimes the idea comes first, and sometimes they come at the same time.

Activity 4.3 Words and concepts

1. What do you think comes first, the word (language) or the idea? Explain.

2. Give an example where the idea or concept exists before the word for it is learned.

3. Give an example where words have helped you to form an idea in your mind.

4. What is an example where the word and idea are created at the same time? Perhaps you can't think of any examples and thus, you believe that words and ideas cannot be created at the same time. If so, why not?

4-3 Requirements to be an official language

Since, in its simplest sense, language is a means for communication, then "body language" is a kind of language. If somebody is standing with his arms crossed and with a frown on his face, that person is sending a message that she or he is nervous or angry. The exact meaning may not be clear, but surely this person is indicating a lack of comfort. Yet, body language is not an official language because it lacks some fundamental characteristics that all official languages share.

Activity 4.4 Non-verbal language

1. What messages can you create with particular body stances, posture, and positions? Give examples.

2. What requests, suggestions, or commands can you give another person without using words? Give examples.

3. What ideas can you communicate with another person without using words? Give examples.

4. Why is "body language" not a "real" language? (You will read about that in the next section, but before you read it, try to answer this question using knowledge you already have.)

4-3-1 Rules

To begin with, all formal languages have a complex set of rules that need to be followed. The fundamental rule for all languages is the way words are ordered to make a statement, command, or question. In this way, American Sign Language (ASL) is a true language because there is a particular order that must be followed when doing "signs" that make up a sentence. These rules are referred to as grammar. For most languages, grammar rules also relate to how words are pronounced and how they are spelled. For most languages, though not all, there are also rules about the way certain words like verbs change according to the time indicated, like the past or the future. There are also rules about the way nouns change if they are meant to be singular or plural. Romance languages, like Italian, Spanish, and French, have "masculine" and "feminine" words with their own particular rules to follow.

Activity 4.5 Language characteristics

1. What are the basic grammar rules of your language?

2. What are the basic grammar rules of English?

3. What grammatical features do you have in your language that don't exist in English?

4. What grammatical features does English have that your language doesn't have?

5. Because of the grammar differences, what is hardest for you when learning English?

4-3-2 Rule evolution

Grammatical rules sometimes change, but usually only in small ways. The larger grammatical rules of a language normally do not change. For instance, English has the basic grammatical rule of putting the subject first, followed by the verb, and then the object. For example, I like pizza. This subject-verb-object order is not likely to ever change. However, smaller grammatical rules can and do change. For instance, for many decades it was taught that when comparing three objects, we use the superlative form: He is the tallest of the three brothers. And when comparing two objects, we use the comparative form: He is the taller of the two brothers. Surprisingly, though, a recent Google search has found that it has become equally common today for people to say and write the following sentence: He is the tallest of the two brothers. This is a grammar rule that seems to have been loosened so that different forms are considered correct. However, this kind of change is rare.

4-3-3 Language change

This brings us to another key feature of language. It is "alive" in the sense that it is always changing. Mainly, this means that old, unused words and expressions slowly disappear from the language, and new words and expressions are always being created. Also, the spellings of a word may change. When a native English speaker tries to read or listen to something written 800 years ago, what we now call Old English, he will soon realize that he does not recognize most of the words, and the spelling will look totally strange to him. In short, without some training and instruction, he will not be able to understand what he is reading. This is because some words no longer exist at all, and many other words have changed their spelling and pronunciation so much as to be unrecognizable anymore.

On the other hand, every year, new words are introduced into a language. Technology and social trends play a great role in creating new words. Since the start of the computer, digital, Internet, and SNS age, a great many number of new words have been created. Fashion trends, leisure activities, and urban attitudes and behaviors all lead to new words. In Japan as well as many other countries, there is even a yearly tradition of announcing the "word of the year", which is the most popular and influential new word created that year. So, although language has certain grammatical rules that are difficult, or even impossible to change, language is still alive in the sense that words are constantly being added or deleted from active use in the language.

It is worth noting that because language is "alive", it can also "die". Many languages of indigenous people around the world have disappeared completely or are in danger of disappearing. An example of a "dead" language that is actually not completely dead is Latin. Nobody uses Latin as his or her native language. It used to be the official language of the Roman Catholic Church, but not anymore. It is not connected to any present ethnicity or culture. And yet, people still study it, read it, write it, and speak it. But these people do so purely as an academic exercise, not for daily communication. Though, studying Latin is a good idea if you want to learn English vocabulary because much of English is based on Latin.

Activity 4.6 Language change

1. Make a list of Japanese words that are no longer or rarely used. These might be words you hear your grandparents speak or words you read in classic books.

2. Make a list of words created by the digital age.

3. Make a list of new words created recently in your language. Classify them as either being based on science, technology, fashion, culture, etc.

4. What was the word of the year last year? What do you think should be the word of the year this year? Make a list of your top five choices.

5. Should "endangered languages" be protected? Why or why not? What practical steps could be taken?

4-3-4 Open-ended language

A final point to be made about language is that it is infinite in its possible combinations. Every day, people make up sentences that have never been spoken or written before. The rules might be limited, but the combination of words is unlimited. It is true that some sentences have been said or written billions of times. A good example of such a sentence is: I love you. In contrast, a sentence like My daughter came home yesterday with a drawing of a dog wearing orange sneakers and climbing a green and purple tree, has probably never been written before.

Thus, we can say language is both finite and infinite in its structure and possibilities.

Activity 4.7 Language's limits

1. In what way is language "infinite"?

2. In what way is language "finite"?

3. Make a sentence that nobody has ever made before.

4-4 The limits of language

Even though we all use at least one language every day, we still cannot use language perfectly. The reason is that language is just a representation of what is in our minds. And so, no language is perfect, and no language can perfectly reproduce what is in our minds. Because of this, we will always have some problems using language for communication. It can be hard to understand what someone is saying, and sometimes we misunderstand others as well.

One problem is clarity. It is often hard to say exactly what we mean, even in our native language. We may understand something perfectly in our minds, like why 25 times 5 equals 125, but if we try to explain it, suddenly we find ourselves getting "tongue-tied", or unable to speak smoothly and clearly.

Another problem is recall. There is the English expression, to have something you want to say "on the tip of your tongue". This means you cannot quite remember the word you want to use. You know the meaning of the idea that you want to express, but cannot quite find the word that matches it.

Yet another problem is simply not being able to express a feeling in words. Maybe you have read or heard the expression, "I cannot say in words how much I love you". Maybe you have said this yourself. The word love exists, but it doesn't feel like it is enough to fully express our feelings. Our emotions and feelings are so complex, with so many layers, that simple words cannot capture the true meaning of what we want to say.

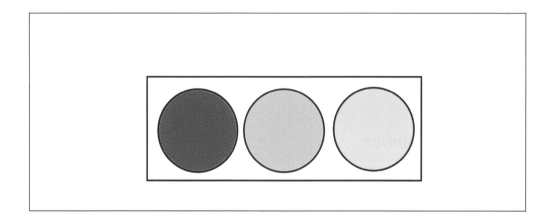

Q: Are the lights of a traffic signal:

A) Red, yellow, green?

B) Red, yellow, blue?

C) Red, orange, green?

D) Red, orange, blue?

Answer: It depends where you're from.

4-5 Ambiguous language

There are inherent ambiguities to language. Let's consider this sentence. "Charlie is rich." The word "rich" is a problem because it's inexact. Is he rich compared to the speaker? Is he rich compared to the other people in the community? Is he rich compared to most people in the world? We have no idea. Thankfully, language has a way of solving this problem. We can say, "Charlie has $10,000,000 in the bank." Then we know what "rich" means in Charlie's case. The problem here is that some words, very often adjectives, have a vague meaning, and so, more explanation is needed.

In another case, the problem is that some words have a double meaning. Consider this sentence: I didn't get your email. The word get has two meanings, which makes the meaning of this sentence ambiguous. One meaning is: I didn't receive your email. The other meaning is: I didn't understand your email. Again, to resolve this, further explanation is needed.

Activity 4.8 Ambiguous meaning

1. Make a list of ambiguous words (hint: many adjectives are ambiguous in meaning).

2. Now, make two or three sentences that are ambiguous in meaning.

3. Now rewrite those three sentences so that they are perfectly clear in meaning.

4. Make a list of words that have a double meaning.

5. Now, try writing at least one sentence that is ambiguous because one of the words has a double meaning.

4-5-1 Language and context

Understanding the meaning of a sentence often depends on context. Consider the following example. "I love that supermarket clerk." Depending on who the speaker of that sentence is, who the listener of that sentence is, and who the supermarket clerk is, that sentence will have a number of different meanings. Is impossible to know the meaning of this sentence without context. Does the speaker mean the supermarket clerk is really good at her or his job? Or does the speaker mean he or she wants to go on a date with that supermarket clerk? Or did the supermarket clerk just make a mistake and accidentally gave too much change to the speaker? We have no idea without context. "Taking words out of context"—that is, taking some words a person said and putting them into a different content than was intended—is thus, a dangerous thing because the entire meaning can be changed. Politicians often do this to each other when debating. News media are often accused of doing this. We'll learn more about that later in this chapter.

Activity 4.9 Words and contexts

1. Make a sentence that is impossible to understand without context.

2. Explain a time when somebody took another person's words "out of context". What was the result?

4-5-2 Intended meanings and surface meanings

Sarcasm can be hard to catch, especially if the sarcastic statement is in written form. Take the following sentences. "That's a nice haircut/car!" "You're so smart!" Can you catch the sarcasm? Probably, you could catch it if you heard it spoken and were well aware of the particular situation. However, if it was in written form, and the context was not clear, it might be hard for you to catch it. Sarcasm is especially hard to catch for people learning a foreign language. A native English speaker learning Japanese might not realize that a Japanese speaker is being sarcastic, and vice versa.

4-6 Translation problems

In English we have an expression: lost in translation. It means that when you translate from one language to another, some part of the meaning will be lost.

People who are involved with translating spoken or written words from one language to another find that there is rarely an exact way to translate a sentence from one language to another. Concrete words like ball, table, and book may be easy enough, although even with such simple words, there may be a subtle shade of meaning that cannot be translated. Once we start looking at whole sentences, it becomes more and more complex, especially when translating between languages from geographically distant places. It is a lot easier, for instance, to translate Spanish into Portuguese, than to translate Spanish into Chinese.

Going further, where literature is concerned, direct translation is nearly impossible. Translators of artistic works like novels, poems, and plays have to make decisions about word choice and shades of meaning. A translator who worked to translate the great Russian poet and novelist Pushkin from Russian into English has stated, "Poetry is essentially untranslatable". That is, if you want to understand the true meanings of a poem, you must read it in the original language. Any translation will be inadequate. Similar remarks have been made of the Japanese theatre tradition of Noh. In a good English translation, a Noh play may be impressive and moving, but in the original Japanese there are so many more connections between words with their secondary meaning. One simply cannot appreciate the depth of poetic echoing in English that exists in the original Japanese.

Activity 4.10 Translation practices

1. Write three complex sentences in Japanese. (A complex sentence is a sentence that contains one dependent and one independent clause.) Now try to translate these sentences into English. What problems do you have in translating?

2. What are some words you feel cannot be translated from Japanese to English?

3. What English words have you learned that you feel you cannot really understand because the true meaning is "lost in translation"?

4-7 Language and media

The media has to be careful what they say or print about someone and the words they use to describe particular events or behaviors. For a respectable and supposedly neutral news source like *The New York Times*, calling a politician a "liar", for example, is a serious accusation, and the editors of this newspaper make great efforts to be certain of the facts before making such a claim. Instead of writing, "Mr. Trump lied", the newspaper may write, "He made a baseless claim", or "His statement is lacking in evidence to support it." The words "baseless claim" or "lacking in evidence" is less severe than "lie" and it leaves room for the fact that perhaps the speaker innocently made a mistake. "Lie" means a deliberately deceptive act, and a conscientious editor will not make such a claim unless she or he is absolutely sure it is true.

4-7-1 Biased language

Today, unfortunately, a lot of media outlets are clearly biased. In the U.S., which has two main political parties—the Republican and Democratic parties—news outlets often have a very clear bias towards one or the other party. Such outlets will be less careful about word choice when accusing a politician from the opposite party. In such cases, a media outlet may purposely print or broadcast information about a politician that has not been fact-checked, is only half true, or is completely false. In these cases, language is being used to unfairly damage, or conversely, to give an unfair advantage to, a particular side. In trying to understand a news broadcast, newspaper or online article, it is good to know what that source's bias is beforehand. That is, if you know that a news source is biased toward liberalism and against conservatism, this will help you see how the facts may be distorted to support that source's political views, and to discount its claims accordingly.

The American TV news channel Fox News, for instance, is famously and blatantly conservative. It will nearly always support a Republican candidate over a Democratic one, and will tend to support a more right-leaning lawmaker over a liberal or even centrist one.

Activity 4.11 News media and language

1. *Name two of the biggest newspapers in Japan. Do these newspapers have a clear conservative or liberal bias? Or is it too hard for you to decide?*

2. *Consider online news sources like Yahoo News or the SNS-based Line News. Do these have a bias? If so, what is their bias? What language is used that tells you that these sources have a bias? What language is used that tells you that this news is intended for a certain age group (under 25 years old, for example, or over 60 year olds)?*

3. *Do you think every media source has a bias? Is it possible for a media source to be completely neutral? Explain.*

4. *Find a newspaper article and try to determine the bias. What words and expressions indicate a bias?*

4-8 Language and Politics

Successful politicians are masters of language. They know how to use language to achieve the desired results. That is, they know what to say, and what not to say, so that people will vote for them.

For one, good politicians have mastered the art of the "non-answer". Did you ever watch a politician give a very long answer to a question and realize that he has just said nothing of substance? Or perhaps, in giving his answer, she or he has simply changed the subject completely. The question might have been about some scandal involving the politician, but the politician gives an answer talking about how terrorists must be stopped. The answer appears to be totally unrelated to the question. Politicians do this all the time. If they don't like the question or know that a direct and truthful answer will cause them trouble, they steer the focus to a different point. Though ethically unacceptable, it's amazing to watch a politician do this, knowing the great skill involved.

Activity 4.12 Political language

1. Write some statements you have heard politicians say. How do these politicians use language so that their statement is purposely unclear?

2.   Consider a press conference or public speech that a politician has given. How does the politician try to appeal to voters? What does he/she say to make potential voters feel good and want to vote for him/her?

4-8-1 Language and responsibility

A more honest politician will try to be as truthful as possible, but even in telling the truth, the politician will be careful about the words he or she uses. During the First Gulf War in 1991, the U.S. did some regrettable actions. President George H.W. Bush, in wanting to be somewhat truthful, made the following statement: Mistakes were made. Consider this sentence for a moment and consider how smart this sentence is. President Bush used the "passive voice" grammatical construction rather than the "active voice". In the active voice, there is a clear subject who does the action. Example: I gave my mother flowers. In the passive voice, the person doing the action may or may not be clear. Example: My mother was given flowers. In the sentence made by President Bush, the doer of the action is not clear. Who made mistakes? We don't know. In this way, President Bush was being truthful and evasive at the same time. Thus, being a smart politician means being very skillful at using language that both reveals and conceals. In some sentences, like "Mistakes were made", information is being revealed and concealed at the same time.

Activity 4.13 Language as a tool of persuasion

1. Make two sentences in which you admit to being guilty of something using the active voice. For example, "I stole $10." The sentences don't have to be true...you are just making examples.

   Now take those sentences and change them to the passive voice so that the actor is not clear.

2. In what other ways can language reveal something and also conceal something? For example, "My partner and I had lunch yesterday." In this sentence, the speaker is revealing that he had lunch with his partner. However, at the same time, the speaker is concealing who the partner is. What does 'partner' mean? Is it a business partner, a romantic partner, a project partner? What gender is the partner? We don't know. My using a vague non-gender word like partner, the identity of the partner is purposely kept unclear.

3. Make a sentence like the above where using a deliberately vague word simultaneously reveals and conceals information.

A successful campaign will also often have a "catchy" slogan. Catchy means short, easy to remember and repeat, and with a memorable message. However, it would be wrong to say that a slogan is simple. When Barack Obama ran for president in 2008, his slogan was "Change We Can Believe In." He even had a chant that people associated with him: "Yes we can." In 2016, Donald Trump used the slogan "Make America Great Again". Both of these men were elected President of the United States, in part because of the brilliance of their slogans. Although these slogans appear simple, they are actually complex. Each slogan contains both a positive and negative message. To analyze these slogans correctly, it is necessary to consider what the slogan is saying about the past, the present, and the future. It is also necessary to consider what the slogan says about the candidate as a person and a leader.

Activity 4.14 Slogan analysis

1. Analyze Barack Obama's slogan. What positive message does it contain? What negative message does it contain? What does it say about Barack Obama as a person and leader?

2. Analyze Donald Trump's slogan. What positive message does it contain? What negative message does it contain? What does it say about Donald Trump as a person and leader?

3. Write down another political slogan (one that you remember, or one that you have found with some research). If it is in your native language, translate it into English as best you can. What are the messages contained in this slogan?

4-9 Conclusion

As human beings, our main method of communication is language. Current research suggests our brains are specialized to process and create language. Language helps us know about the world, and gives us the ability to contribute new knowledge to the world. It is important to remember that language is not a perfect tool, though. There are some things we cannot express just with language, and sometimes we misunderstand what others are trying to express to us. Being more thoughtful about the language we hear and use will help us sharpen our knowledge and keep us well informed about the world around us.

R.G.

Chapter 5 Sense Perception

5-1 Introduction

How do we get information? How do we interact with our surrounding environment? Well, the most basic answer to these questions is that we get information through our senses. We use our senses to interact with our environment. A baby, for example, before being able to use language, is able to get information, or learn about its environment, through the senses. All animals use their senses to get information about their environment, to find food or to sense danger. We could say that we humans use our senses to connect with our surrounding environment, the outside world. It is with our senses that we perceive and get knowledge about the world.

Indeed, according to *empiricism*, all knowledge must be based on perception and experience. In this textbook, we will not follow this somewhat extreme idea. We will instead argue that there can be other sources of knowledge apart from sense perception. However, it is certainly true that our senses are an important source of knowledge.

According to common-sense realism, our senses give us a true perception of reality. In other words, the world is pretty much as we see it. This would mean that our senses work well. Of course, if our senses didn't work well, we would probably not be able to survive, neither as individual humans nor as a species.

It may be that in everyday life, this kind of understanding is adequate. In most situations, our senses do indeed give us a fairly good picture of reality. However, we are studying knowledge in this textbook, and in this section we are studying the senses as a source of knowledge. Therefore, it is necessary for us to look a little deeper into the topic. In this way, we will try to find out if common-sense realism is indeed true. Do our senses always give us a valid picture of reality?

In this chapter we will investigate the different senses to determine if indeed sense perception is a reliable source of knowledge. We will also try to find out if some senses are more reliable than others, as well as whether some senses are more important than others. We will look at ways in which our senses can be tricked, meaning ways in which our senses can make mistakes about reality. Furthermore, we will look at ways in which our senses can be improved using technology. We will conclude this chapter by looking at how we can confirm the information about the world that our senses give us.

5-2 The Senses

How many senses do humans have? Well, the answer seems simple, doesn't it? We have five senses: sight, smell, sound, taste and touch. However, there are in fact more than these traditional five senses. Here are some of them: the ability to sense temperature (called *thermoception*), the sense of balance (*equilibrioception*), the sense of vibration (*mechanoreception*), the ability to sense the position of our limbs, such as our hands (*proprioception*), and the sense of pain (*nociception*). While these senses are interesting and important, in this chapter we will focus on the traditional five senses: sight, smell, sound, taste and touch.

5-2-1 Hierarchy of the senses

Are all of these five senses equally important? Are some senses more important than other senses? Probably many people think that sight is our most important sense. We get lots of information visually, through our eyes. We have a number of phrases that support the idea that sight is an important sense. For example, we say, "seeing is believing", and "I'll believe it when I see it". Both of these phrases connect sight with knowledge. We don't for example say, "hearing is believing", or "I'll believe it when I smell it". Why is this? Is sight really the most important sense?

Activity 5.1 Evaluating the senses

1. Which senses are more important for you and which are less important? Make a list with the most important sense at the top and the least important at the bottom.

2. Imagine that you had to lose one sense. Which sense would you give up? Why?

Did you choose to give up the sense of smell? Was it at, or near the bottom of your list of senses? It seems that many people would choose to give up the sense of smell. This must mean that many people think smell is the least important of the five senses.

Activity 5.2 Experimenting with your senses

Try eating chocolate while holding your nose, and then let go of your nose. How is it different? Try the same thing while drinking a cup of coffee or tea.

But, when you're eating, which sense is more important? The human tongue can distinguish (recognize) only five different types of taste: sweet, sour, salty, bitter, and *umami* (savory). However, the nose can distinguish many more different types of smell. How many different smells do you think the human nose can detect? Recent research has suggested that the human nose can distinguish over one trillion different smells, or odors. That is 1,000,000,000,000 different smells! Doesn't this mean that our sense of smell is much more powerful than our sense of taste? Well, anyway, it certainly shows that much of the pleasure of eating actually comes from our sense of smell.

While there is no doubt that our five senses work very well (the sense of smell being a good example), they have some limitations. Our senses do not pick up all the information from the world around us. Our eyes for example, do not work so well at night, they do not see ultraviolet or infrared light. Our ears also can hear only certain kinds of sounds, called audio or sonic. Our ears cannot hear ultrasonic sounds (frequencies higher than audio), or infrasonic sounds (frequencies lower than audio). Our sense of sound also doesn't work very well under water. Sound travels faster underwater and it is difficult for the human ear to find out where sounds come from underwater. As we said before, our sense of taste can recognize only 5 different tastes. How do human senses compare to other animals?

5-2-2 Sense perception in other animals

We all know that dogs' sense of smell and sound is much better than humans'. Police, for example, use some dogs to smell out illegal drugs or explosives. Some dogs are also used to track people. Dogs use much more of their brain to analyze smells than humans do, and probably this is one reason why their sense of smell is much better. Dogs can also hear sounds of a much higher frequency than humans, and this is why humans cannot hear a special type of dog whistle that is designed only for dogs to hear. However, on the other hand, humans' sense of sight may be much better than dogs. Some researchers think that dogs can only see in black and white, and shades of gray.

Some other animals have completely different senses. Bats and dolphins have echolocation. They can make sounds that bounce off objects around them. The sound waves then reflect back to the animal, which can use that information to judge the size, shape and distance of that object to themselves. The human inventions of radar and sonar use this principle. Radar was developed during World War II as an early warning system. It uses radio waves that bounce off approaching aircraft. These radio waves then reflect back to the radar station, which can detect the approaching aircraft. Sonar in submarines uses sound waves in the same way as dolphins.

Birds have a magnetic sense, which enables them to migrate for thousands of miles. The Arctic Tern holds the record for the longest migration. Amazingly, every year, it migrates from one pole to the other, enjoying the southern summer in the Antarctic and the northern summer in the Arctic. A recent study has found that the Arctic Tern travels about 70,000 km a year. It seems likely that birds like this can sense the magnetic field of the earth.

Snakes have a strong sense to detect heat, meaning that they can sense the body heat of another animal. This means that snakes can hunt at night, and can find and kill their prey using this strong sense of heat detection. Snakes also have a very good sense of smell, using their forked tongue.

Sharks have electroreception, which is the ability to sense electric fields. They can detect the electric fields of other animals. Some sharks have very sensitive noses and it is believed that this is where the sensors are located for picking up electric fields. Sometimes sharks are attracted to the motors of boats because these motors have electric fields.

5-2-3 Improving our senses with technology

We said before that our senses have limits. However, we have also seen that humans have extended or improved their senses by using technology. Sonar is a example of this. With sonar, we can "see' underwater into the far distance. Radar is also a technology that enables us to "see" far-off things. In what other ways can technology improve our senses? Well, microscopes help us to see tiny things, atoms and subatomic particles. In the opposite way, telescopes help us to see into the far reaches of space. Of course, in our everyday lives, glasses and contact lenses help us to improve our vision. Google glasses take this idea a step further, by providing extra information about our surroundings. This information is much more than just what we can see. It is information that has been collected from a large number of sources. Obviously, such devices should dramatically improve the knowledge we can build from our senses.

Medical science also uses technology to see into the human body. This began with X-rays, using radiation to "see" the inside of the body. MRI (Magnetic Resonance Imaging) uses magnetic fields and radio waves to produce an image of the inside of the body. This image is far superior to the image produced by X-rays.

It seems that we are on the verge of another computer revolution. Computers will soon become so advanced that they will become AI (artificial intelligence), able to learn, adapt and sense! It may be that these computers will be able to see, hear, smell, touch and taste in ways similar to humans.

There are many other ways that we have been able to improve our senses with technology. These technologies make our senses better. This means that our senses are then able to get more information from our surroundings, and this should increase our ability to create knowledge. However, is it possible that our senses can sometimes make mistakes? Can our senses be tricked?

5-3 Senses and Knowledge: Illusions

When we ask the question of whether or not our senses can make mistakes, or be tricked, we are really talking about *perception*. Our senses are only part of the process of perception. We could say that our senses provide us with the sensation of interacting with the world around us. In this way our senses provide us with the information about the world around us, or reality. Our brains then interpret this information. In other words, our brains try to understand the information provided by our senses.

We don't usually think about how our brains interpret the information given by our senses, because interpretation happens automatically. However, as we are studying how our senses affect knowledge it is important to look at this process. We are going to look at illusions to investigate how our perception can misinterpret the information given by the senses. These illusions will show us how our brains can become confused by the information. Our brains are then unable to interpret, and in this way our brains can make mistakes. Basically, our brains can be tricked!

5-3-1 Context

One example of an illusion is the Ponzo Ilusion, named after the Italian psychologist, Mario Ponzo. The Ponzo Illusion shows how the brain judges the size of an object according to the background, or the context. In the picture we can see train tracks  with two yellow lines. Our brains judge the length of the yellow lines according to the train tracks and this means that our brains think the upper yellow line is further away. Therefore, we perceive the upper yellow line to be longer. If you check with your ruler, you will find out that both yellow lines are the same length. We could say that our brains have been tricked into perceiving a 2D picture in 3D.

5-3-2 Figure and ground

When we look at something we tend to look for figures, or objects, and we tend to ignore some parts as ground, or background. It means our brains are trying to identify figures that it knows. The Profile/Vase illusion is a very good example of this. Our brains can interpret this as either a symmetrical vase, or as two faces looking at each other.

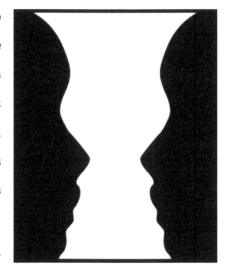

The two images of the Young lady-Old lady and the Young man-old-man are also the same. Can you see both the old and the young? Sometimes it helps to blur your vision slightly.

Incidentally, there is also a phenomenon called the Moon Illusion. Have you ever looked up at the moon and thought that it looks bigger than normal? Well, sometimes the moon does appear bigger, and this is because of its elliptical orbit around the earth. However, the moon also appears bigger when it is closer to the horizon and this is called the Moon Illusion. Scientists disagree as to why this occurs.

Of course the key point with these illusions is that they show that our brains can be tricked. They show the importance of interpretation to the process of perception. This is important for us because this interpretation happens in the same place as knowledge is built: in our brains.

5-4 Our unconscious brain and perception

Psychologists have been experimenting on the role of our unconscious in perception. Many have proved that the unconscious mind does indeed have an important role in perception. Scientists have shown that the unconscious brain plays a role in gathering information from our senses. They have also shown that the unconscious brain is important in decision-making, as well as perception. *Subliminal messaging* is an example of this. Subliminal messaging uses the unconscious brain's ability to perceive. Importantly these images are outside the ability of our conscious brain to perceive. However, this does not mean that we do not perceive such images. It means we perceive them in a slightly different way. Subliminal messaging is not usually legal in advertising, but one interesting study found that people who watched an episode of "the Simpsons", which included subliminal messages of the word "thirst" or a picture of a can of Coca-Cola, were indeed thirstier after watching.

5-5 Selectivity of Perception

So, we have seen how perception can be mistaken, and we have seen how our senses can be tricked into making mistakes. This shows us that we should be careful about how we interpret the information our senses give to us. However, there is another important thing that we need to investigate. Our perception is selective. This means that even though our senses get vast amounts of information from the world around us, our brains select what information is important and what information is not important. We could say that our brains focus on the most relevant information, and ignore the other information.

It seems that humans are more likely to perceive moving objects. Obviously, this is part of our biological evolution. In the past, an object moving towards us could have been coming to eat us!

5-5-1 Selecting according to Interests

We may select what we perceive according to our interests. For example, if you are thinking of getting a new Smartphone, you will suddenly begin to take notice of the different Smartphones that you see around you. Likewise, if you are interested in trains, when you go to a major station you will perceive all the different types and models of trains. Someone else at the same station may not notice any of that, and may be just looking for the train to take them home. Small children are intensely interested in nature and they will walk along the street and notice the different colors and shapes of the leaves on the ground. Most adults will not even notice the leaves.

Activity 5-3 Memories of selective perception

1. *Are there some important things that you did not notice on the first day you came to university?*

2. *Think of an example of when your perception changed because your interests changed.*

5-5-2 Selecting according to emotions

Perhaps it is obvious that our emotions affect our perception. If we are in a good mood, we tend to focus on the good things in the world around us. If however, we are in a bad mood, we tend to focus on the bad things in the world around us. We could say that we perceive things that support our emotional condition. Likewise, we ignore things that contradict, are opposite to our emotional condition. When we fall in love, we tend to see only the good things in our partner's character. When we fall out of love, it is the opposite: we tend to see only the bad things.

5-5-3 Change Blindness

Because our perception selects, or chooses, what information is important, we can sometimes experience change blindness. There have been some very interesting experiments that show that our perception will ignore important information if it is not expected. This means that we sometimes do not perceive something important if it is not what we are focusing on.

There are two experiments, in particular, that show this phenomenon. Both of these can be found online.

1. A person is talking to a stranger, but they are interrupted for a short time when two people walk between them carrying a big wooden board. At this

time, the person cannot see the stranger. Amazingly, many people don't notice when the first stranger is replaced by a second, different-looking stranger. About 50 percent of people just keep talking to this new stranger as though nothing has changed.

2. An audience is asked to watch a video of a group of people throwing a basketball to each other. The audience is asked to count the number of times the basketball is passed. Amazingly, most people don't notice the man in the gorilla suit who walks across the screen in front of the group of people passing the basketball.

It may be that in each of these two experiments, people are focusing on a task, and don't expect the change. Because the change is unexpected, our brains ignore the information.

5-6 Checking our Perception of Reality

We have learnt how our senses can be tricked. In this way, our senses can make mistakes about the world around us. We've also learned that our perception can also be mistaken. We sometimes don't perceive important things because our perception is selective, meaning that our brains choose what is important and what is not. So, what should we do about this? If our senses and our perception can make mistakes, should we trust them? Well, the answer is of course, yes, we should trust them, but it is safer if we double-check. But, how do we double-check?

5-6-1 Double-check with another sense

One way to double-check is to use another sense to confirm. For example, if something looks like an apple and tastes like an apple, then it is very likely that it is indeed an apple. If we go outside on a cold morning, and the ground looks icy, then we can carefully test it with our feet to see if it really is ice. When we boil some water to make a cup of tea, we wait until we see steam coming from the saucepan, and hear the sound of boiling water. We are using two senses to double-check the information. Of course, if we want to be really sure that the water is indeed hot, we could touch the saucepan, although this action could result in a burn!

5-6-2 Does it fit?

Another way to double-check our perception is to consider whether the new information 'fits' with our experience of the world around us. If some new information does not fit with our experience of reality, then there is a good chance that we are mistaken. There is a phrase in English, "when pigs fly", which means 'impossible'. We know that pigs cannot fly. They have no wings, and are not shaped aerodynamically. So, if we one day saw a pig flying over our house, it is likely that we would not think it was actually a flying pig. We would likely think it was a balloon, or a dream.

5-6-3 Check with someone else

Yet another way to double check the information our senses receive is by checking with another person who is with us. If one person sees something unusual and then tells their friends about it, it is possible that their friends would not believe them. But, if ten people saw the same unusual thing and then told their friends about it, it is much more likely that people would believe them. This can be called a kind of independent testimony. In this case, someone else independently confirms the new information received by our senses. This makes it considerably more reliable. In fact, we often do this when we are with other people. If we see something dramatic or interesting, we will turn to our friend and say, "did you see that?" When we say this, we want our friend to confirm that they too have seen the same thing.

5-7 Conclusion

We began this chapter by looking at the different senses. We discussed whether some are more important than others. We then looked at the senses of other animals and found that many animals have senses that we humans do not. But, we then discussed how humans are able to use technology to both improve our natural senses, and to give humans new senses.

Following on from this, we looked at perhaps the most important part of this chapter, which is how our senses can make mistakes about reality. We found that our senses can be tricked, or become confused. This is because of the process of perception, which happens in our brains and not in our senses. Our brains can misinterpret the information given by our senses. Importantly, our brains can also select which information is important and which is not important. So, this means that the information we perceive with our senses is not 100% safe. It is generally safe, but we need to be careful. Finally, in this chapter we looked at ways that we can double-check, or confirm, the information we receive from our senses. Using these methods we can make our perception more reliable.

P.S.

Chapter 6 Reason

6-1 Introduction: Everyday reasoning and formal reasoning

What is reasoning? How is it useful to help us know about the world? How much certainty can it give us? What kinds of reasoning errors are common? This chapter considers these issues. This may sound abstract, but consider the following cases.

A. For almost the entire year, professor X has never worn a suit and necktie to class. And then one day she does. You decide that it must not be a regular day for professor X, but a special day in some way.

B. You have a dog, Z, at home. It always barks at strangers. You hear someone come into the house, but the dog doesn't bark. You figure that whoever came into the house must not be a stranger.

C. In history, every human being has proved to be mortal. The greatest age any living person has achieved is around 122 years. Since we—the authors of this text and the students using it—are human, we reckon that we will die too, one day.

These are all examples of everyday reasoning that use *deduction*. They take some general ideas about how the world is, and apply them to particular events or cases.

We can see that they all have a similar structure. There are two statements concerning something we know about the world. The first statement is more general and the second is more precise. They lead to a third and concluding statement that must be true, given what the first two statements state. A deductive argument that has this structure is known as a *syllogism*.

6-1-1 Syllogisms

Premise 1 (general)	Premise 2 (particular)	Conclusion (P1 + P2 = C)
(A1) X always dresses casually.	(A2) Today, X is dressed formally.	(A3) Therefore, today must be a special day in some way for her.
(B1) Z always barks at strangers.	(B2) Someone came in and Z didn't bark.	(B3) It must have been someone Z knows.
(C1) All humans are mortal.	(C2) We are all humans.	(C3) We will die one day.

In formal logic, the two statements of a syllogism are known as premises. The first, more general statement is the major premise, and the second more particular statement is known as the minor premise.

For another example, take the following.

(P1) No married people are bachelors. (General statement)

(P2) Jane is married. (Particular statement)

(C) Therefore, Jane is not a bachelor. (Logical conclusion based on P1 and P2)

A syllogism has two more characteristics for us to note. Firstly, it has *three terms*—in this case "married", "bachelor", "Jane"—that each appear twice. It also has *quantifiers*, or words that specify "how many" or "how much". In this example, the quantifier is the "No" attached to "married people", which tells us that no person can be a bachelor if they are married. Other common quantifiers are "all", "some", and "most".

This kind of logical reasoning can give us certainty about knowledge. Such certainty cannot be obtained from other ways of knowing. If the first two premises of a syllogism are correct, then the conclusion must be correct. No matter what you believe or what values you hold or where you come from, this conclusion will always be correct, in the same way that one plus one always equals two for all people in all cultures and in all times of history. Because of this chance of certainty, some people, often called rationalists, believe that reason is the best and most important way of knowing.

Activity 6.1 Senses versus reason

If your senses told you one thing, and your reason told you something else, which would you trust? In answering, try to think of some examples of this kind of conflict.

Do you agree that logical reasoning is universal, or that it is the same everywhere for everyone? Or do you think it may be different according to time and place and person?

6-1-2 Truth and validity

Statements or premises can be said to be true or false. A conclusion too, may be true or false. But in formal logic, the *truth* or falsity of statements is not the key issue. Rather, the most important issue is whether the overall structure of a syllogism—the overall argument—is *valid*.

To be valid, an argument must have a conclusion that follows logically from the premises. It doesn't matter whether the premises are "really true", or not. You could have an argument in which both of the two premises and the conclusion were all false, and it would still be valid so long as the premises justified the conclusion!

6-1-3 Examples of valid arguments

P1: All swans are white. *P2: That bird is a swan.* *C: That bird is white.*	*Note that the first premise is not true: there are black swans in Australia. But despite being factually mistaken, this is valid as a logical argument.*

P1. All teachers are aliens. *P2. Noah is a teacher.* *C: Noah is an alien.*	*It is unlikely that the first premise is true. The conclusion also may be untrue. But this argument is valid because its premises justify the conclusion.*

6-1-4 Examples of invalid arguments

All dogs are mammals. *Lassie is a dog.* *Therefore Lassie is not a mammal.*	*This cannot be a valid argument, since the premises do not justify the conclusion. To be valid, it should say:* Therefore, Lassie is a mammal.

All humans are mammals *All whales are mammals.* *Humans are whales.*	*This one too, has two true premises, but the conclusion does not follow from them. All you could reasonably conclude in a valid manner is:* Therefore, humans and whales are both mammals.

Activity 6.2 Syllogism creation

Create some syllogisms that are valid and which fit the following conditions:

A) Two true premises and a true conclusion P1: P2: C:	Example No humans are hamsters. Russell is a hamster. Therefore Russell is not a human.
B) One true premise, one false premise, and a true conclusion P1: P2: C:	Example All students are human. Patrick is a student. Therefore Patrick is human.
C) One true premise, one false premise, a false conclusion P1: P2: C:	Example All humans are mortal. That robot is human. Therefore that robot is mortal.
D) Two false premises and a true conclusion P1: P2: C:	Example All men are women. Masa is a woman. Therefore Masa is a man.
E) Two false premises and a false conclusion P1: P2: C:	Example All humans are hamsters. That robot is human. Therefore that robot is a hamster.

6-2 Why focus on argument structure?

It may seem strange to you that formal logic is concerned more with an argument's validity than with its truth. After all, isn't truth what we should be looking for? Well, there are a few reasons for this focus on structure. Simply, the first is that "absolute truth" is not accessible to us through our ways of knowing. Perception, emotion, language are the basis of logical reasoning, but all of them are fallible. In other words, we cannot trust any of them 100%. However, rationalists figure that we can be 100% sure about validity. Rationalists think it is important to have some knowledge that we are 100% sure about.

A further reason for focusing on structure is the fact that it helps us to overcome biases that affect our thinking. For example, we often have belief bias, which is to agree with an argument not because it is well argued, but because its conclusions match what we already believe. Conversely, we might disagree with an argument not because it is badly argued, but because we don't like the conclusion.

If we take arguments and think about them using formal logic, we can examine them more objectively, and consider whether it is a rational argument that we should agree with.

Activity 6.3 Turning real-world debates into syllogisms

Choose one of the following. Research one argument for it, and one argument against it. Then reduce each argument to a syllogism, and consider whether each one is valid.

1) Changing / not changing Article Nine of the Japanese Constitution.

2) Using / not using nuclear power to generate electricity.

3) Increasing / not increasing Japan's refugee and immigrant intake.

6-2-1 Determining validity

To tell if a syllogism is valid, you can draw a Venn diagram that sets out the relationship between the three terms in the first two premises. This shows you whether the conclusion is justified or not.

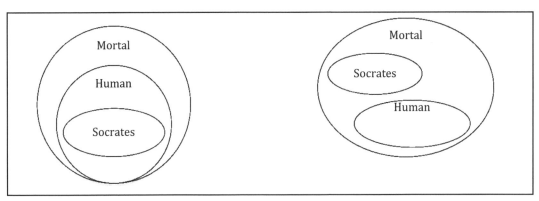

All humans are mortal.
Socrates is a human.
Therefore Socrates is mortal.
Valid

All humans are mortal.
Socrates is mortal.
Therefore Socrates is a human.
Invalid

Activity 6.4 Drawing Venn diagrams

Draw Venn diagrams for the following, and state whether they are valid or not.

A) All human beings are mortal. Zeus is not mortal. Therefore Zeus is not human.

B) All otaku have rucksacks. Buffy has a rucksack. Therefore Buffy is an otaku.

C) All trees have leaves. Roses have leaves. Therefore Roses are trees.

D) Pigs can't fly. Babe is a pig. Therefore Babe can't fly.

E) All Italians eat spaghetti. Leonardo da Vinci eats spaghetti. Therefore, he is an Italian.

F) All acrobats are brave. Some brave people are kind. Therefore some acrobats are kind.

G) Some monks are Indian. All Indians are good at yoga. Therefore some monks are good at yoga.

Next, take a moment to consider how you could change the invalid syllogisms to make them valid: in many cases, adding or removing a word may be enough!

6-2-2 Incomplete arguments

When we use or encounter reasoning in everyday life, it is often simplified. Especially, things that seem obvious are often left out, because we assume others already understand those things. An argument with a missing premise is called an *enthymeme*.

Activity 6.5 Completing incomplete arguments

Supply the missing premise in the following examples.

1) "If it's Borden's, it's got to be good." (Borden Ice Cream advertising slogan)

P1:

2) "He is ill, since he has fever." (Aristotle, Rhetoric*)*

P1

3) "My parents decide to buy my brothers BB guns. Because I am a girl, I do not get a gun." (Alice Walker, Beauty*).*

P1:

4) "We were attacked on September 11, so we went to war against Iraq". (George W. Bush, 2003, paraphrased)

P1:

5) "The gun has the defendant's fingerprints on the trigger. He is clearly guilty!" *(Corbett and Connors,* Classical rhetoric for the modern student*)*

P1:

6) "People who don't smoke cigarettes are better risks than people who do. People who are better risks deserve better rates." (State Mutual Life Insurance)

C:

6-3 Inductive reasoning

Deductive reasoning begins with general statements, applies them to particular cases, and comes to a conclusion. You have to keep in mind, however, the fact that it is only useful if your general statements are correct, and your knowledge about particular cases is also correct. If you're wrong, then your reasoning may be valid, but completely untrue!

The famous syllogism about humans being mortal, Socrates being a human, and Socrates therefore being mortal, is only useful to us if it is true both that humans are mortal, and that Socrates is human. How do we know that humans are mortal? Well, basically, the answer is that we are sure of this because of experience and observation. Everybody so far in history has died.

The Population Reference Bureau in Washington D.C. estimates that perhaps 107 billion people have been born in the last 50,000 years. They have all died. Based on this huge number of people who have all died, we generalize that all human beings are mortal. This kind of reasoning, which goes from the particular to the general, is known as *inductive* reasoning.

If every ice cream you've ever eaten has been sweet, you will expect that trend to continue in the future. You may be happy to state that "all ice creams are sweet", just as "all lemons are sour". These statements are based on inductive reasoning. If you've never seen any lions on the streets of Kyoto, then your experience should make you happy to agree with the reasoning that there are no lions in Kyoto. Basically, in the case of inductive reasoning, we assume that the world is regular and orderly. We expect that what has been true in the past for us will continue to be true in the future for us. Induction, as the above discussion may have suggested to you, is quite reliable, but it is not 100% certain.

Activity 6.6 Induction and generalization

1) Say we receive a large box containing 100 mandarin oranges (mikan). Unfortunately, all 10 in the top row are rotten or moldy. It looks like the next row down too, is rotten. How many would you think it is necessary to check before you give up and decide that they are all rotten?

2) How many times would you want to visit a particular restaurant, in order to decide if it is a great place to eat?

3) Metals expand when heated. How many metals would you like to check of the 91 listed on the periodic table, before you are happy to accept that this is true?

4) What percentage of smokers would need to develop lung cancer, for you to decide that cigarettes are absolutely and undoubtedly bad for you?

6-3-1 Deduction and induction compared

Deduction, based on general statements, gives us certain knowledge about particular cases. Induction, based on generalizations from many particular cases, gives us less certain but broadly applicable knowledge.

Deduction	Induction
General rule	*Observation of many particular cases*
Humans are mortal.	X, Y, Z all died.
Particular case	*Find pattern / tendency*
Socrates is human	All humans in history died.
Conclusion	*General rule*
Socrates is mortal	Humans are mortal.
More certain, but less informative	Less certain, but more informative

You may notice, however, that it is not really true that one type of reasoning provides better knowledge than the other. Rather, we should say that deduction is based on induction. As you can see in the table above, the general rule that humans are mortal depends on induction and the many billions of historical examples of mortal humans.

Activity 6.7 Evaluating arguments

Decide if the following examples are inductive or deductive, and if they are deductive, decide whether they are valid or invalid.

1) *All Republican presidents have been in favor of a strong military. President Trump is a Republican president. It follows that President Trump is in favor of a strong military.*

2) *Tomo is on the softball team and has short hair. Danae is on the softball team and has short hair. Kenji is on the softball team and has short hair. It seems likely that all the members of the softball team have short hair.*

3) *All members of Soka Gakkai are Buddhists. Setouchi Jakucho is a Buddhist. So, she must be a member of Soka Gakkai.*

4) *If Terry were the serial killer, then her fingerprints should be on the gun. Her fingerprints were on the gun. Therefore, it is clear that Terry is the serial killer.*

5) *Most Japanese Prime Ministers did not die in office. Therefore, it is doubtful that the twelfth Prime Minister of Japan died in office.*

6) *Paying terrorists to get them to release hostages is not a wise policy, since that will only lead them to take more hostages in the future.*

7) *For the past 50 years, it has always rained more than 100 centimeters a year. Therefore, it will probably rain more than 100 centimeters this year too.*

8) *Since Tom is the brother of Agatha, and Agatha is the mother of Raquel, Tom must be the uncle of Raquel.*

6-3-2 Induction and reliability

It may seem likely that all humans so far, all humans now, and all humans in the future have been, are, and will be mortal. But not all general statements based on inductive logic are this reliable. Often, we generalize without enough evidence. Having met a few American people and watched some US movies, you may make some generalizations: Americans are X, or Americans are Y. Having seen some groups of Chinese people on the streets of Kyoto and seen media reports about them, students may generalize that Chinese are A, or Chinese are B. However, these are likely to be hasty generalizations, which involve bad reasoning.

Activity 6.8 Hasty generalizations

1.   *Give three examples of a hasty generalization.*

2.   *Do you think people are quick to generalize about others? Why or why not?*

6-3-3 Problems with generalization

Firstly, the sample size is too small in these cases. It is unreasonable to make claims about hundreds of millions of people, or more than a billion people, just based on a few encounters and some media products. Not only that, the sample is almost certainly biased. The people encountered personally are not likely to be representative of any general population in terms of wealth, occupation, education, gender, political beliefs, family background, and so on. Such hasty generalizations are unjustified and can easily lead to prejudiced stereotypes. While stereotypes may be useful for making jokes, they are not at all useful as a source of knowledge.

This risk of being affected by mistaken and stereotyped thinking is increased by confirmation bias. Once we begin to believe something, we tend to notice things that fit with our beliefs more than things that contradict our beliefs. Once we think that we know that Americans are X, or that Chinese are A, we are likely to notice only supporting evidence, and to ignore contradictory evidence. This can make it hard to overcome hasty generalizations.

Finally, even generally reliable generalizations can be wrong. It's not always true that water boils at 100 degrees. If you add salt or sugar, then the boiling point will be higher. Very sweet water containing 90% sugar, for example, won't boil until you reach 130 degrees. To take another case, there are only white swans in Europe, so Europeans believed that all swans were white. That was until they discovered that there are black swans in Australia. We must keep in mind that inductive knowledge is provisional, and that exceptions or new knowledge can make us change our knowledge.

Activity 6.9 The Cash Register exercise

Read the following story. Below it there are 12 statements about the story. After you read the story, determine whether each of the 12 statements is: 1) T – true, 2) F – false, 3) U—uncertain (there is not enough information to say whether the statement is true or false).

The Story

A businessman had just turned off the lights in the store when a man appeared and demanded money. The owner opened a cash register. The contents of the cash register were scooped up, and the man sped away. A member of the police force was notified promptly.

12 Statements about the Story

1. *A man appeared after the owner had turned off his store lights.*	
2. *The robber was a man.*	
3. *The man did not demand money.*	
4. *The man who opened the cash register was the owner.*	
5. *The store owner scooped up the contents of the cash register and ran away.*	
6. *Someone opened a cash register.*	
7. *After the man who demanded the money scooped up the contents of the cash register, he ran away.*	
8. *While the cash register contained money, the story does not state how much.*	
9. *The robber demanded money of the owner.*	
10. *It was broad daylight when the man appeared.*	
11. *The story concerns a series of events in which only three persons are referred to: the owner of the store, a man who demanded money, and a member of the police force.*	
12. *The following events in the story are true: someone demanded money, a cash register was opened, its contents were scooped up, and a man dashed out of the store.*	

Adapted from William V. Haney (1973), "The Uncritical Inference Test", in *Communication and Organizational Behavior: Text and Cases.*

6-3-4 Good generalizations

Good generalizations should be based on a decent number of samples. For a tourist to say, "Japanese people are polite", just because they meet five or ten people who are polite to them, is a generalization that is based on insufficient cases.

To continue with this example, it is also likely that the kinds of Japanese people a tourist meets are not diverse enough. Generalizations must be based on a wide range of representative samples. Tourists mainly meet workers in restaurants and hotels and convenience stores. Such workers are necessarily polite, because the level of service in Japan is so high. To make a generalization about Japanese people as a whole, it would be necessary to consider sufficient numbers of people from all family backgrounds, occupations, levels of education, genders, sexual orientations, ethnicities, political leanings, and so on.

Further, to make sure that your generalizations are not just prejudice involving confirmation bias, you should also look for exceptions to what you think is a general case. Anyone who wants to claim, "Japanese people are very polite", had better actively search for cases of people being rude, uncaring, passive aggressive, violent, and so forth.

When accepting any generalization, it is probably a good idea to require more evidence if it is a surprising claim. If it is coherent with other things that we think we know, then we can probably accept it with somewhat less evidence. The claim that "Japanese people are ruder than people elsewhere" would require quite a lot of evidence before being accepted. By comparison, the claim that "Japanese people working in service industries are usually polite" may be accepted with less evidence.

Finally, it is clear that generalizations in the human sciences are much less reliable than generalizations in the natural sciences. Done properly, chemical reactions always lead to the same result. But human affairs are not like that. People are constantly changing, sometimes from day to day, or even from minute to minute. Opinion polls about politics, fashion, musical tastes, and morality even, show that people change their opinions, which means that human science generalizations are often unreliable.

6-4 Reasoning errors

People make mistakes in their reasoning everyday, and in many different ways. Such errors can be found in private conversations, media reports, academic essays, and political statements. In order to help you avoid making these errors, and to prevent you from believing bad arguments, we will discuss a few of the most common types of errors.

Errors of reasoning are known as *fallacies*, and there are many different types. The errors that you can see by looking at validity are *formal fallacies*. Errors that only become visible when you look at the contents of claims are known as *informal fallacies*. To illustrate the difference, look at these two cases.

- *All bullfights are cruel and savage. All executions are cruel and savage. Therefore, all bullfights are executions.*

  This argument commits a formal fallacy, in that its format is all As are B, all Cs are B, therefore A = C. You don't need to examine the meaning to determine whether it is wrong or right: it is invalid. To confirm this, just replace the A with dogs, the B with animals, and the C with cats: it can't work. But the following example is different.

- *The Tokyo Sky Tree is made of atoms. Atoms are invisible. Therefore, the Sky Tree is invisible.*

  As a matter of formal logic, this argument is valid. But if we look at what it claims, it is obviously mistaken: atoms may be invisible, but large buildings are not.

The problem in this argument is not validity. Formally, it is valid. But in terms of meaning, it is not: it contains an *informal fallacy*, that things are the same as what they are made of. Each atom may be invisible to the naked eye, but the larger things that atoms are made of are visible. Such errors or informal fallacies come in a wide range of types. Below, we consider some of the most important.

6-4-1 Arguments against (for) the person

One of the most common but powerful informal fallacies is the ad hominem fallacy, which is an argument against (or for) the person, rather than their reasoning. Typically, the structure in the negative case is something like this: Person X believes that argument A is true. Person X is not a good person. Therefore, argument A must be false. In the positive case, it would be like this: Person X believes that argument A is true. Person X is a good person. Therefore, argument A must be true. In both cases, the justification given for the conclusion is not the reasoning, but the character (good or bad) of person X.

Thus, to dismiss Abe Shinzo's comments about Japanese colonial era and wartime atrocities for being biased on the grounds that he is the grandson of a war criminal would be to make an ad hominem attack that is not based on reasoned criticism of the content of his statements. Similarly, those who reject Donald Trump's ideas because they think he is racist, sexist, and ethnocentric are also making the same error: they are attacking the person, rather than the person's ideas.

6-4-2 Arguments from ignorance

A second type of fallacy that we have already briefly discussed is the argument from ignorance, or the *ad ignorantiam* fallacy. This is when a person knows that nothing is known or proven about a topic, and then makes an unjustified conclusion. *Scientists have not been able to prove that X exists. Therefore, we can be sure that it doesn't*. Alternatively, *Scientists have not been able to disprove the existence of X. Therefore, we can be sure that it exists.*

Infamously, Joe McCarthy used this logic in the United States during the early years of the Cold War. He tried to find communists in important positions in American society. He said about one person, "there is nothing in the files to disprove his Communist connections", and then he went on to conclude that the person must be a communist! In other words, lack of proof that the person was not a communist was claimed to be proof that the person in fact was a communist. Such arguments from ignorance are typically made by security agencies and militaries, which like to claim that the fact that there is little evidence of other countries' aggressive intentions is no reason not to believe that they have them!

6-4-3 Circular reasoning

An argument suffers from the fallacy of circular reasoning if it assumes the truth of what it is trying to prove. *Sleeping pills make you sleepy, because they are sleeping pills.* The first part refers to the second part, but the second part refers back to the first part again. It's a circular argument.

Religious arguments often show this kind of circularity. *The greatness of the existing world is proof that God made it. Therefore, we know that God exists.* The idea that the world is a great place is used to say that god made it. This idea is then used to argue that god must therefore exist. Since the second part is explained by the first part, and the first part is explained by the second part, this argument is circular.

6-4-4 Equivocation

The fallacy of equivocation occurs when a key word is used several times, but with different meanings. From a comic

strip: *"Hey! You can't just take that! It's stealing." "So what? They steal in baseball all the time. If it's OK for baseball players to steal, logically it's OK for me to steal too."* Stealing things that belong to someone else is morally and legally questionable. Stealing bases in baseball, or advancing on a pitch, may not make the defending team happy, but it is not often considered to be morally wrong (in the early 20th century, there was a debate, incidentally, about the morality of baseball in Japan for precisely this reason). In this dialogue, however, the two meanings are mixed up It is a clear case of logical equivocation, used for comic purposes.

A mouse is an animal. Therefore, a large mouse is a large animal. In this also amusing case, the equivocation concerns the term large, which means different things depending on its context. If it modifies the noun "mouse", then it means large for a mouse. Mice are usually quite small. But when it modifies the noun "animal", then it is in relation to *all* animals. Water buffalo, elephants and hippos are large animals. Thus this example mixes up these two meanings of "large", and so commits the fallacy of equivocation.

6-4-5 False analogy

False analogy fallacies claim that 2 things that are alike in one way are alike in other ways too. *People who have to have coffee before they can function are just the same as alcoholics who have to have a drink in order to function.* This example says that people addicted to coffee are similar to people addicted to alcohol. Certainly, both are dependent on a chemical substance. However, the two addictions are not really comparable. Being addicted to alcohol tends to make you less capable of regular everyday social interaction and work. However, being addicted to coffee does not have a major negative impact on your productivity and relations with others. Most people would claim the opposite: Caffeine improves your ability to work and to communicate with others. To say that dependence on coffee is as bad as dependence on alcohol is to make a false analogy: the two things are alike only in terms of dependency, but not in other important ways.

6-4-6 False dilemma

When someone asks you to choose between two options, even though there are actually more than two choices, they are putting you in a situation with a false dilemma. Consider the case of energy policy. Nuclear energy comes with long-term and uncertain risks associated with accidents, leakage, waste storage, and disposal. Fossil fuel powered electricity comes with CO_2 emissions, air pollution, and also leads to financial gains for authoritarian governments in the various non-democratic states that export oil and gas. These are real problems. But if someone claims that we have to choose one or the other, then they are setting up a false dilemma, since there are a number of other choices: We could choose both options, or neither options, or one or the other plus a range of alternative renewable energy supplies, for example. To pretend that there are fewer choices than there really are is to pose a false dilemma, which is an error of reasoning that we should be careful about.

6-4-7 Hasty generalization

The hasty generalization is another informal fallacy that we have briefly discussed. The problem is generalizations that are based on insufficient evidence. *A poll of voters in the capital showed that the governing party and the main opposition party are currently equally popular. Therefore it is likely that the next election will lead to a stalemate in the parliament.* This statement may, at first, seem reasonable. And yet, if this was about a country like Japan or the United States, for example, it is clearly a hasty generalization. Why? This is because people in capital cities, e.g., Tokyo or Washington D.C., are not like people in regional cities or in rural areas. How Tokyo or Washington people vote cannot be used as a good guide to how people in the rest of the country will vote. The grounds for making this generalization are insufficient; it is a hasty generalization.

6-4-8 False cause

Another common fallacy involves arguing, with insufficient proof, that there is a causal relationship between things. *I broke a mirror, and then I had a bicycle accident. It must be true that it's bad luck to break a mirror.* Well, the connection between breaking the mirror and having a bicycle accident is time: the mirror broke before the bike accident. But that doesn't mean that there is a causal relationship between them. Breaking the mirror didn't cause the accident, and to pretend that it did is to commit the fallacy of false cause.

A variation of the false cause fallacy occurs when you say that something is caused by one thing, when in fact a range of things causes it. *Students' writing and reading skills and general knowledge are improving every year. Clearly, our teachers are doing a great job.* However, the problem is that teaching is not the only factor that affects students' abilities. A wide range of factors must be involved. Therefore, if the credit is given to just one factor—teaching—then this becomes an example of a false cause fallacy.

A further variation of the false cause fallacy is known as the *slippery slope fallacy*. Doing X, for example, is claimed to lead to Y, even though there is insufficient evidence to believe this. Since Y is undesirable, doing X should be avoided. *If we are not strict on soft drugs, then drug users will move from those soft drugs to harder drugs, and we will have a more serious drug problem.* This is a common argument used in arguing for a crackdown on drugs. But it does not seem to be based on much evidence. Beer drinkers do not seem predestined to drink wine, then sake, then whisky and *shochu* and vodka, and then ethyl alcohol. Nor do smokers of low tar and low nicotine cigarettes necessarily move on to regular filtered cigarettes, and then to unfiltered high tar and high nicotine cigarettes. Why users of other drugs would constantly seek "harder" drugs is not established. Thus this is a case of the slippery slope fallacy.

6-4-9 Special pleading

To be inconsistent in an argument is considered to be an informal fallacy. For example, if you say that certain rules or standards should apply in one case, but not in another similar case, then unless you have very good justifications, it is likely that you are using special pleading. *"Yes, I do think that all drunk drivers who cause fatal accidents should go to prison, but not my daughter! She is a good girl who just made a single mistake!"* The emotional reason for not following the rules in this example—*not my daughter!*—is understandable, but not acceptable as a reason for ignoring the rules. So, this is an example of special pleading.

Students asking for an extension on an essay claiming that they are busy with work for other classes are also likely to be using special pleading. All students will have a similar amount of work to complete in the same amount of time. In such a case, a student would need to have proof of exceptional circumstances so as not to commit this fallacy.

6-4-10 Other common informal fallacies

Appeals to force (ad baculum): *You will be punished / hurt / harmed if (unless) you do X. So you had better not (had better) do it.*

Appeals to pity (ad misericordiam): *If you do (don't do) this, you will cause terrible suffering to A and B, so you shouldn't (should) do it.*

Appeal to the people (ad populum): *Everyone's (No one's) doing it, so you should too (shouldn't either).*

Accident: applying a general rule to a case it is not designed to cover: *You should keep your promises. When X married Z, X promised to stay with Z for life. Therefore, X should stay with Z now, even though X has become a violent drug-abusing gambler.*

Activity 6.10 Identifying informal fallacies

1. *At the trial, the burglar said he saw the politician kill his wife. The politician claimed that you couldn't possibly trust a burglar, who was by definition dishonest, so that his testimony should be ignored.*

2. *"President Reagan was a great communicator because he had the knack of talking effectively to the people."*

3. *Happiness is the highest good for a human being, since all other values are inferior to it.*

4. *A: "I've never heard him talk about any girlfriends." B: "Well, he must be gay then."*

5. *Evolution is obviously true. We see it happening all the time.*

6. *"A criminal trial is like a professional sports match. The only important thing is winning."*

7. *In the end, you'll have to get married to him, or break up.*

8. *I've read four test papers so far, and they were all really good. I think this year's students are so much better than last year's.*

9. *If voluntary euthanasia is made legal, it will not be long before involuntary euthanasia is introduced.*

10. *That the Korean economic miracle occurred was all thanks to Japan's*

colonial infrastructure program.

11. *You know, the countries that eat the most chocolate have also won the most Nobel prizes. Obviously, chocolate makes you smarter.*

12. *The US and France and the UK all have nuclear weapons, but North Korea and Iran shouldn't be allowed to have any.*

13. *The famous environmentalist Lester Brown says that the destruction of tropical rain forests is one of the ten most serious worldwide problems. Thus, it must be the case that this is indeed a very serious problem.*

14. *No one would buy a pair of shoes without trying them on. Why would anyone get married without living together first?*

15. *Many Japanese politicians are being investigated for illegal fundraising activities. We obviously can't trust them to do a good job, since they're clearly dishonest.*

16. *You shouldn't try to limit what people say. People have a right to free speech.*

17. *I know the deadline was yesterday, but the question was very difficult, and I had a cold.*

18. *Murder is bad, and murderers need to be punished. But I only murdered James because he was mean to me, and I was drunk.*

19. *Philosophy helps you argue better, but do we really need to encourage people to argue? There's enough hostility in this world.*

20. *Since the class has no questions concerning the topics discussed in class, the class is ready for a test.*

21. *In spite of all the talk, not a single flying saucer report has been authenticated. We may assume, therefore, there are not such things as*

flying saucers.

22. *"No one objects to a physician looking up a difficult case in medical books. Why, then, shouldn't students taking a difficult examination be permitted to use their textbooks?"*

23. *Why should cracking down on terrorism help to stop it, when that method hasn't worked in any other country?*

24. *My wife had a car accident. Women are such dangerous drivers.*

25. *My grandfather smoked and drank until he was 94. Smoking and drinking can't really be that bad for you.*

N.M.

Chapter 7 Emotions

7-1 Introduction

Yet another way of knowing is through our emotions. In many ways, emotions are the opposite of the previous way of knowing we studied, reason. In using reason, we are using logic. Also, we are considering the order of things, their causes and effects. In short, we are thinking. With emotions, our reactions are immediate. Thinking may cause us to feel a particular emotion. Or, feeling a particular emotion may cause us to think. But, emotions themselves are not thoughts. They are feelings. Even so, we can say that emotions help us understand ourselves, and the world around us. In this way, they help us to know about the world.

There is an expression in English, "Ignorance is bliss." It means, not knowing about certain things will make you a happy person. If you didn't know about the wars, suffering, poverty, cruelty, deception, and unfairness in the world, you might be perfectly happy. Of course, to be 100% ignorant of the reality of the world is impossible. However, some people are more ignorant than others. Yet, ignorant is not a positive word. It means you are lacking key knowledge about something or about the world in general.

Activity 7.1 Is ignorance desirable?

1. *Do you agree with the statement "ignorance is bliss"? Would you rather be ignorant and perfectly happy, or well informed and not as happy? Explain your answer.*

Activity 7.2 Colors and emotions

1. Often, colors are connected to specific emotions. Look at the following three examples. What does each sentence mean? Why do you think certain colors represent certain emotions?

I'm seeing red.	
I am green with envy.	
I feel blue.	

2. What other expressions do you know, that use color to indicate emotions?

7-1-1 The emotions and reason

The truth is that reason and emotion cannot be so easily separated. Sometimes reason comes first. Sometimes emotion comes first. Sometimes they are so closely connected that it is hard to distinguish which comes first. Whatever the case, emotions and reasons have a deep connection. Let's consider the following sentences:

- *After hearing the news that my friend was going to move to another country, I became sad.*

- *When the plane made a sudden drop due to turbulence, a wave of fear came over me.*

- *I started laughing the moment I saw my friend because by chance she was wearing the exact same Mickey Mouse T-shirt as me.*

In the first sentence, clearly reason has come first. My friend told me she was moving away, and I thought about this. I quickly deduced the fact that I would not see my friend for a long time. This idea of not seeing my friend for a long time is a conclusion made from my reasoning ability. My reasoning led me to feel sad.

In the second sentence, my fear came immediately after something scary happened. While it may be true that my brain quickly computed that I was in danger, the emotion of fear happened so quickly that it could be said to have come first. Only afterwards was I able to reason what had happened and evaluate the danger thoughtfully.

In the third sentence, it is again possible that reason came first. My brain had to understand that my friend was wearing a Mickey Mouse T-shirt, and then I had to remember that I was wearing a Mickey Mouse T-shirt, and then I realized that we were wearing the same thing. However, it all happened so quickly that the realization and the emotion happened almost at the same time.

In this way, it can be said that emotion and reason are inseparable. This is a key connection because it means that we can "reason ourselves into sadness" and also "reason ourselves into happiness". For example, perhaps we have just had a good day. Everything seems to be going well. The sun is shining, it's a holiday, and you just had a great dinner with some of your friends. You go home happy, but on the way home, you start thinking about all the people in the world who are suffering, all the refugees and innocent victims of war. You think, "It's not fair!" This thinking makes you feel sad. On the other hand, you may have just failed a test, and you just broke up with your lover. Then, you lost your wallet! Wow…you are having a really bad day. But then you think about all the people in the world who have far worse lives than you: people who work for one dollar a day; people who have lost family members due to terrorist attacks. Then you reason that your life is not so bad, and you ought to be grateful for all that you do have. In this way, you are able to make yourself happy. Or, at least, you are able to make yourself "less sad".

As humans, we do this all the time. It is this ability to use reason to regulate our emotions that make it possible for us to function in daily life, and to develop as human beings. If we could not do this, we would remain like babies who cannot control their emotions at all.

Activity 7.3 The contexts of emotions

1. *First, make a list of as many situations as you can that require reason. For example, answering questions on a test requires reason.*

    Second, make a list of as many situations are you can that involve emotion. For instance, if you left your umbrella on the bus and then you got soaking wet because it was pouring rain outside, you would feel angry.

    Finally, make a list of situations where both reason and emotion are involved. For instance, if your father yelled at you for coming home at 2am, you would at first feel some emotion, maybe fear or sadness or anger. At the same time, you might be using your reason and thinking why he was yelling at you.

2. *Do you think reason always comes before emotion, or do you think it is possible for emotion to come before reason? Explain.*

3. *Are there any cases where you can feel pure emotion with no thought involved, or does emotion always have to be connected to a thought?*

4. *Give an example of an occasion when you "reasoned yourself into" some emotion.*

7-1-2 Basic emotions

For over 2,500 years, Western thinkers have been trying to determine how many emotions humans have. The Greek philosopher Aristotle (384–322 BC) believed humans have 14 emotions. These are: anger, mildness, love, enmity, fear, confidence, shame, shamelessness, benevolence, pity, indignation, envy, emulation, and contempt.

Much more recently, the great thinker Charles Darwin (1809-1882) developed the theory of evolution, which contained arguments about the universality of human emotion. Emotions, just like other biological features, evolved over time. They are biological adaptations of the human race, just like walking on two feet.

In the 1970s, studies by psychologist Paul Ekman (b. 1934) seem to confirm Darwin's evolution-based notion of universal emotions, which linked facial expressions to emotions. Dr. Ekman co-developed the Facial Action Coding System (FACS), which tracks the number of muscles involved in different facial expressions. Results from his experiments seem to indicate that all humans share six basic emotions. They are: anger, happiness, surprise, fear, disgust, and sadness. Later, Dr. Ekman's studies led him to add a seventh universal emotion: contempt.

Each emotion is attached to a particular facial expression. Look at the pictures below. Can you tell which of the seven basic emotions is being expressed in each picture? Please try before reading further.

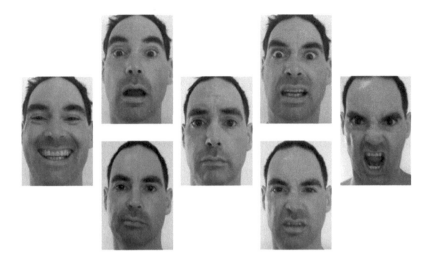

Seven basic emotions

Now that you have guessed each of the emotions, before we look at the answers, let's consider the expressions connected to each emotion more exactly. For happiness, the lips are turned upwards and the cheeks are raised. For anger, the eyebrows are lowered and the lips are usually tightened. Disgust is close to anger, but with disgust, the nose is often wrinkled and/or the upper lip is raised. For contempt, one side of the mouth is turned upwards, and the other side of the mouth looks like a frown. Sadness is expressed by the inner part of the eyebrows being raised, and usually the lips are turned downwards. Surprise and fear are also similar, but with surprise, the mouth is often open with the lips making an "O" shape, and the eyebrows are raised. With fear, the mouth may also be open, but eyebrows are lowered. After reading this, you may want to look at the pictures again and see if you want to change your guesses.

Another famous psychologist, Robert Plutchik, concluded that humans have eight basic emotions, with many more secondary emotions. According to Dr. Plutchik, the basic emotions are: anger, anticipation, joy, trust, fear, surprise, sadness, and disgust. In 1980, he created a wheel of emotions, which shows the different intensity of basic emotions. In this wheel, the emotions in the middle circle are the basic ones. The emotions in the inner circle are the higher intensity of the basic emotions, and the emotions in the outer circle are the lower intensity. Take anger, for example. In the lower intensity, anger is just annoyance. In the higher intensity, anger becomes rage. Take some time to view the wheel and note the differences in intensity.

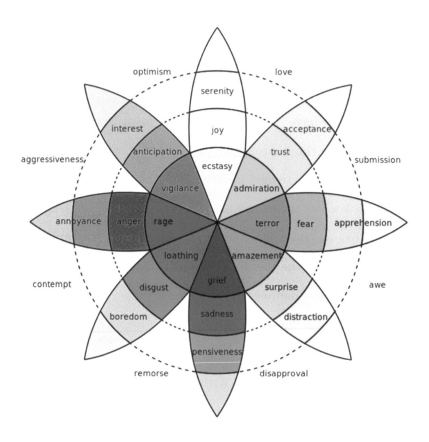

Plutchik's Wheel of Emotions (*Wikimedia*)

However, a study published in 2014 by Dr. Rachael Jack at the University of Glasgow suggests that there may only be four basic emotions: fear, anger, happiness, and sadness. Her research suggests disgust is really just the same as anger, and surprise is really just the same as fear. These results are from a different way of measuring facial expressions that seem to indicate there are only four different types. These results are debatable, though, and research in the subject of emotions is continuing.

7-1-3 Secondary emotions

The above discussion revolves around what may be considered basic emotions. However, most people would agree that humans have dozens of "lesser" emotions, which we can call secondary emotions. Among these would be emotions like bittersweet, which is a feeling that combines the basic emotions of happiness and sadness. When something is bittersweet, it has some elements that make you happy but other elements that make you feel sad. If you think about a happy memory you shared with your ex-lover, for instance, your memory would be bittersweet. The bitter part, of course, is that the person is no longer your lover.

It could be argued, though, that secondary emotions may not simply be the combination of two or more basic emotions. They are more varied and complex than that. For instance, consider the emotion of nostalgia. Yes, we could say that nostalgia is a combination of happiness and sadness, but it seems more specific than that. It is a feeling about a happy time in the past that no longer exists, and because it no longer exists, you feel sadness. Like this, humans have a wide range of complex emotions, many of them connected to a very specific situation and connection between past, present, and future events in our lives.

Activity 7.4 Theorizing about emotion

1. Which theory do you agree with most? How many basic emotions do you think we have? Four, six, seven, eight, fourteen, or even another number? Explain why you think so.

2. Aristotle identified "love" as an emotion. Do you agree? Is love an emotion? Or, is love a combination of different emotions? Or is love something different from emotion?

3. Make a list of secondary emotions. Try to list as many as you can, and share with your partner or in a small group.

4. With your partner, or in a small group, analyze the list of emotions you have compiled. Analyze and try to explain the meaning of these emotions. Which emotions are simply a combination of the basic emotions? Which are more than just a combination of basic emotions? Explain.

7-2 Emotions: differences between cultures

Let us consider Darwin's assumption again. He believed there were six basic emotions, and furthermore, that these emotions could be universally understood through facial expressions. In other words, we have six basic emotions and six basic facial expressions to show those emotions. It is a matter of human biology and nothing more. Darwin believed that no matter where you are from, you can understand if another person is happy, sad, or filled with disgust just by looking at the expression on her face.

Let's also consider Dr. Rachel Jack's experiments again. These experiments seem to indicate that the expression of emotion is shown and perceived differently based on a person's cultural background. In one of her experiments, both Western (Caucasian) and Asian participants recognized a smile as an expression of happiness. However, other emotions were not as easy to distinguish. The Caucasian participants basically recognized Darwin's six basic emotions and corresponding facial expressions. The Asian participants, however, clearly identified only the emotions of anger, fear, surprise, and disgust. Thus, it appears from these experiments that emotional expressions are based on culture.

If emotional expressions are based on culture, then it would also be reasonable to assume that particular emotions can vary by culture. The six basic emotions are likely universal among all cultures and peoples. Everyone gets sad and cries. Everyone gets happy and laughs. Depending on the culture, some people might get angrier and be more likely to show anger than other people.

But, how about more subtle emotions? These can vary from culture to culture. We know this because there are certain emotion words in a language that are not easy to translate into another language. In fact, it may be said to be impossible to accurately translate some emotion words. Take, for instance, the Japanese word wabi-sabi. A Japanese person would have a hard time translating this into English, and likewise, an English speaker would have a hard time understanding this word. However, if a native English speaker visited a traditional Japanese temple garden with a Japanese friend on a grey, cloudy day, the Japanese friend might be able to "guide" the English speaker into understanding the emotion of wabi-sabi. Thus, it could be said, understanding emotions from culture to culture requires some context, rather than just an explanation using words. Finally, the fact that the English speaker could learn what wabi-sabi means, and in turn actually have the feeling of wabi-sabi supports the idea that human emotions are universal. We all have the capacity to feel the same emotions. What is different is the way some cultures shape and craft particular emotions so that they seem unique to that culture.

Does this photo convey *wabi-sabi?* If yes, why?

If no, what emotion do you feel from this photo?

(Image by Russ Garofalo)

Activity 7.5 Translation practice

1. For those of you who are native Japanese speakers, try to translate wabi-sabi as best you can. Tell your translation to a native English speaker. Can he or she understand you based only on your words?

2. Make a list of secondary or subtle emotion words that exist in your native language.

3. Take three of these words and try to translate these words into English. Do not give up. Even if it is difficult, try to reach a reasonable translation of these words.

4. Evaluate your translations. On a scale of one to ten, rank your translation. How good are they? One means it is not good at all, and can't be understood. Ten means it is great and perfectly explains the emotion.

7-3 Emotions and knowing

Having considered the universality of emotions, it is time to look at a deeper question: Why do humans have emotions?

If you were a Darwinian biologist or evolutionist, you would have an easy answer to this question. We have emotions because they help us survive. Furthermore, not only do we have emotions, but we also have great differences in the degree or intensity of our emotions. That is, sometimes we feel a little scared, and sometimes we feel terrified. Sometimes we feel a little annoyed, and sometimes we are furious. All of these emotions have a biological foundation. We feel emotions because of our physiology: our brains, nervous systems, memories, and abilities to critically analyze a situation and react in a way that will keep us alive.

Emotions are essential for us to know about the world. One of the earliest physical responses a baby makes is called the "moro reflex". When a baby feels that she is falling or if a baby hears a loud noise, she will tighten her body, throw her arms into the air, and also likely clench her fists. This is a physical reaction that could be described as primal fear. The baby is scared because she feels threatened by something from the outside world. She can't even sit yet, or crawl, or walk, or talk, but she feels fear. From this we could say that fear is "built into" our bodies, and that there is a close connection between pure feeling and physical response. In fact, they are inseparable.   We know because we feel. Or is it, we feel because we know? That is a hard question to answer, but let's just say these are inseparable things. Feeling helps us to know, and knowing helps us to feel.

Many people are afraid of snakes. There is a good reason for that. A snake is hard to see, very fast, and will bite you if you startle it. Their bites are painful and can be deadly. It is smart to be afraid of snakes. If you saw a rattlesnake at your feet and you weren't scared, you're likely to get in big trouble. Being scared is good: scared of certain animals, scared of certain places like a stormy ocean or windy cliff, scared of certain people who may do you harm. Ignorance is not bliss in this case. Ignorance of the evil intentions of some people, or the dangers of nature, can lead to death.

Activity 7.6 Emotions and survival

1. What are some animals you are afraid of (most people are afraid of more than one animal)? Why are you afraid of these animals? How does being afraid of these animals help you in your ability to survive?

2. What are some nature places or situations you are afraid of? Why are you afraid of these situations? How does being afraid of these situations help you in your ability to survive?

3. What is a situation when you saw a person who made you feel scared? Where were you, and who was it? Why were you scared? How did being scared help you?

4. Imagine an emotion meter that ranks emotions from 1 to 10, with 1 being a weak feeling and 10 being a strong feeling. A ranking of 1 for anger, for instance, would be mild irritation or annoyance. A ranking of 10 for anger would be rage. When have you felt a 1 about something? When have you felt a 10? Consider a few situations in your life, and the emotions you felt. Give these emotions a ranking depending on the situation.

5. In each case (related to the previous question), how did your emotions help you learn about yourself, the situation, and/or the world? That is, what did your emotions teach you? Explain.

7-3-1 Emotions and ethics

A special way in which we may learn from our emotions is in the case of ethics, or social awareness. For example, if we see two people violently fighting in the street, we might feel sadness, fear, surprise and/or disgust. These feelings are a spontaneous reaction to what we are seeing. Depending on what feeling we have, we will learn something. Perhaps seeing this fight makes us feel disgust. From this we may confirm a social or moral principle that we have already learned, like fighting is wrong.

However, deeper learning may also occur. Perhaps your reaction is in opposition to the reaction that others around you are having. Maybe, for example, you saw some kids bullying another child. All the kids seem to be enjoying bullying the child. They are smiling and laughing. But you do not think it is funny. It makes you sad. It makes you disgusted. Even though the social situation seems to be telling you that this behavior is "OK" or even "fun", your emotions are telling you a very different truth: it is not OK. Thus, what is happening in society and what we feel inside ourselves is sometimes different. In this case, your emotions are guiding you to the correct way to behave and treat others.

Activity 7.7 Emotions and ethical truths

1.   *Explain an experience you have had where your emotions pointed you to an ethical truth. Was this ethical truth the same as what others around you seemed to believe, or was it in opposition to what others seemed to believe? Give details.*

7-4 Emotions and socialization

Furthermore, there is the fact that a facial expression such as a smile might mean different things in different cultures. In some cultures, for instance, people sometimes smile when they are angry. In this way, a smile is not a reflection of happiness, but rather a socialized response used to hide a completely different emotion, anger. In some cultures, also, a person may make a look of confusion or surprise when really the emotion they are feeling is disgust. If you are from New York, you usually have a good idea when somebody is angry at you. They furrow their eyebrows, tighten their lips, and wrinkle their noses (and usually say something nasty, too!). If that same New Yorker visited Kyoto, he might not realize when somebody is angry at him. People from Kyoto make very subtle expressions, in contrast to New Yorkers. The Kyoto-ite's face may appear 'blank' to the New Yorker, though another Kyoto-ite could immediately tell that the person is angry. In this way, facial expressions are social behaviors that are learned, and they differ from culture to culture.

Activity 7.8 Emotional universality

1. Do you think emotions are universal? Explain your answer.

2. Do you think emotional expressions are the same for all cultures and can be understood by everyone in the same way? Explain your answer.

3. Have you ever smiled when you were angry? What was the situation?

4. What is another facial expression that can be misunderstood? In other words, you feel some emotion, your make a facial expression, and somebody misunderstands the emotion you are feeling. Actually, this happens very often. Think of at least one example when you have experienced or seen this happening.

7-4-1 Emotions - innate, learned, or both?

You don't need to learn to cry!   **Smiling is learned behavior.**

Right from birth, a baby cries when it is upset. However, it is said that a newborn "learns" to smile at around 6 weeks old. It is debatable whether a baby "learns" to smile or whether it is innate. Young children show frustration, a form of anger, by screaming, crying, and refusing to do what their parents want them to do. You may have gone to the supermarket and seen a toddler sitting in the middle of the aisle crying with his mother standing over him and begging him to "be good".

As babies grow into children and children grow into adults, they learn more and more about facial expressions. They learn which ones are appropriate in some situations and which ones are not appropriate. Think of some facial expressions you have learned to hide your emotions or convey a particular message.

Activity 7.9 Facial expressions

1. How many of your facial expressions are natural and how many are the result of social conditioning.

2. Think of some facial expressions you have learned to hide your emotions or convey a particular message.

7-5 Emotions and reality

Emotions can filter how we perceive things, similar to the way a pair of sunglasses color what we see. If you wear a pair of rose-colored sunglasses, everything will appear rose colored. If you wear a pair of blue-colored sunglasses, everything will appear blue. Similarly, if we are angry, we might perceive an event or experience differently than if we are happy. For instance, suppose you are in a bad mood because you got up late and had to hurry to catch the bus. It is raining and you forgot your umbrella, too. Once you get on the bus, you might get more easily annoyed by the people on the bus than you normally would. Perhaps someone near you on the bus is listening to hip-hop music so loudly on his or her headphones that you can hear it. Actually, you like hip-hop music and normally this wouldn't bother you, but on this day, since you still feel anger from having to hurry, this situation might make you even angrier. On a different day, you got up early, had a delicious breakfast, heard some great news on your favorite SNS application, and it was a sunny day. When you get on the bus that day, you might happily listen to the hip-hop music coming out of a nearby person's headphones. It all depends on your mood.

The above example is quite simple and clear, but such types of reactions can be much less direct and have subconscious roots. For example, you are having dinner with your good friend, when this friend, who often jokes around with you, says a sarcastic comment to you, as she or he has done many times in the past. Though you often tease each other, this time you are suddenly very hurt and saddened by the comment your friend made. She or he was only joking, which you often do, but this time you took it seriously. Later, when you think about this event and regret reacting so negatively. In reflecting about why you reacted in such a way, you may be reminded that earlier that day, in the morning, you read an article about a child who was bullied in school and the terrible things other children said to him. Though you didn't really think too deeply about it at the time, this information was stored in your memory and influenced the way you reacted to your friend's comment. You might then realize just how affected you were by the article. It made you sad but this sadness was quickly repressed. Your friend's comment brought out the emotion that had been hiding in your mind.

Activity 7.10 Shared emotions

1. *Share an experience where an emotion affected your reaction to an event in a negative way.*

2. *Share an experience where an emotion affected your reaction to an event in a positive way.*

3. *Share an experience where you had an unusual reaction to something that you have experienced many times. Try to trace this reaction back to its root cause. Also, notice how repressed emotions can be brought out by certain events.*

7-6. Emotions and the body

As we have seen above, emotions are mental processes. That is, our feelings are affected by our thoughts. When we start thinking about something happy, we become happy. It is also true that emotions can be purely the result of physical stimuli. When we get into a nice warm bath, we instantly start to smile and feel happy and relaxed. The water has had a soothing effect on our body, and consequently, our mind. On the other hand, if you have a pebble in your shoe, and you continue walking for a while, you will soon get annoyed and angry. The physical irritation soon becomes emotional irritation. In this way, how we feel physically affects our emotions. Numerous studies have examined, for instance, the way sleep affects our emotions. Those who get eight hours of deep sleep tend to be happier than those who can't get enough sleep or whose sleep is interrupted by noises or other factors. Health experts all agree that exercise is an important ingredient for happiness. If you exercise, your body will be healthier, and you will feel happier as a result.

A researcher named Jonathan Balcombe published a study that claims that even for animals like fish, there is a connection between the body and emotions. His study notes how some fish come up to divers and swimmers to be 'petted'. Being petted feels good, and leads to what we would call a 'happy' feeling. Of course, we have to be careful when talking about animals and emotions, and we shouldn't be too quick to state that animals have emotions that are the same as ours.

Activity 7.11 Actions and emotions

1. *What is a physical action that makes you feel happy? Explain.*

2. *What is a physical action that makes you feel angry? Explain.*

3. *If you are feeling sad, what physical action can you do that will change your mood to happiness?*

4. *If you are feeling nervous, what physical action will calm you down?*

5. *Try to recall all the things you do daily that are actually an attempt to change your mood.*

7-7 Conclusion

Emotions, at first glance, may not seem to be a way of knowing. They are feelings, and as such, they are different from knowledge. However, as we have seen in this chapter, emotions are, in fact, a very powerful way of knowing about the world. They are closely connected to reason (and thus, language), and help us form an understanding of our past, our present, and our future. We need emotions to evaluate things that have happened before, things that are happening now, and things that will happen soon or in the distant future. Are we safe, or are we in danger? Is someone being treated well or badly? The questions to these questions come from our "gut", a word that means an immediate emotional response. We have the saying: Trust your feelings rather than your thoughts. More wisely, perhaps, is the fact that emotions are used along with other ways of knowing to keep us well informed about the world around us at all times.

R.G.

Chapter 8 Personal and Shared Knowledge

8-1 Introduction

What is personal and shared knowledge?

In this chapter, we will look at two different kinds of knowledge. One is personal knowledge and the other is shared knowledge.

Personal knowledge is knowledge that you can gain from your everyday experiences. For example, you might know how to make a tasty dish because you have cooked it so many times. This kind of knowledge is called first-hand, personal knowledge. In contrast, shared knowledge is knowledge that you can get from other people. It can be from your family, community, culture, school, Internet, the news media and so on. This shared knowledge is called second-hand knowledge.

Of course, these two kinds of knowledge complement each another. For example, maybe you can speak English fluently because you learned it at school (shared knowledge). However, you surely also spent many hours practicing by yourself (personal knowledge).

In this chapter, we will focus on why shared and personal knowledge are important for us. We will begin by looking at major sources of shared knowledge. Then, we will think about the importance of personal knowledge.

8-2 Sources of shared knowledge

Shared knowledge is important, simply because the majority of our knowledge is shared knowledge. Such knowledge is passed on from one generation to the next, from one society to another, and from one individual to another. How is knowledge shared? In this chapter we will look at five different ways in which knowledge is shared: the Internet, cultural tradition, school, the news media, and expert opinion.

8-2-1 The Internet

Recently, most of us use the Internet every day, and it has changed our lifestyles in many dramatic ways. Compared with books, we can get a lot of information instantly. We could also say that the amount of information on the Internet is almost infinite, or endless. Moreover, a lot of people use smart phones these days. So, many people can access an almost infinite amount of information anytime anywhere.

You can also be the source of information by setting up your own websites or blogs, or by posting your opinions to online discussion forums. In this way, with the Internet, anyone can become the source of information for many other people. If we think about this, we can see that we should be very careful about information we find on the Internet. Obviously, we cannot say that all information on the Internet is correct. So, we should always think about how we can decide which information is reliable and which is not. How could we distinguish the information we believe in from the information that we do not?

Activity 8.1 Internet information

Imagine that you find the following two articles on the Internet. Which one do you trust more and why?

Article A: "Women nearly twice as likely to have money as men"

The most up-to-date research shows that women are nearly twice as likely to have money as men. A research conducted by Mr. John Beerlover, a researcher living in Cambridge, revealed economic gaps that exist between men and women. He interviewed a total of 45 people in his town, 15 men from his poor neighbourhood, and 30 women from Downton Street, one of the wealthiest areas in the town. Mr. Beerlover remarked that, "this finding shows that gender inequality is already solved in this country, and what is more, this study suggests that women should pay twice as much tax as men".

Article B: Malaria mosquitoes are as attracted to Limburger cheese as to human foot odour

Bart Knols, a professor at Wageningen Agricultural University in the Netherlands, discovered that the female malaria mosquito is attracted equally to the smell of Limburger cheese and to the smell of human feet. This discovery was published in one of the most prestigious medical journals, the Lancet (volume 384, number 9, 1996). This suggests that next time you go camping in Africa, you should bring some Limburger cheese and put it just outside your tent. The malaria mosquitoes will not bother you, and you will have no more sleepless nights!

8-2-2 Cultural tradition

Our beliefs and practices are passed on from our ancestors in the form of culture. This means cultural tradition is also a source of our knowledge. Cultural traditions and the knowledge we get from them can have a very strong influence on the way we see the world. Cultural traditions influence what we think of as 'normal' or 'reasonable'. We often call these 'norms', and they are very important.

Norms are basically rules about accepted and unaccepted behavior, defining the "normal" ways of doing things. They are accepted and followed by almost all people within a society.

Importantly, we often don't think critically about norms. This is because we are often not formally taught about norms, but just follow what other people in our society are doing. These norms are also connected to the way we see the world. Norms, and the way we see the world are also very closely connected to our common sense. Since there are many cultures in the world, common sense in one culture is not always common sense in another.

Activity 8.2 Norms at university

1. At university, what are some things that students are expected to do (required actions)? What are things that students are not expected to do (unacceptable actions)?

2. Are there differences between students in different departments and faculties? How about between students at different universities? What about at different universities in different countries?

Some people say that the Internet is reducing cultural diversity and making all cultures more similar. For example, imagine that all people in the world access the same kinds of information every day on the Internet. Given that information shapes how we see the world, all people, regardless of their local culture, could end up acquiring very similar ways of seeing the world. This worry is maybe exaggerated, but it is understandable.

At the same time, however, the opposite worry is also expressed sometimes. The Internet is so varied and so diverse that many people only look at specific things that interest them. Online, there are millions of communities of people interested in topics as diverse as *Gundam* plastic models, anarchic politics, or Kenyan pop groups. As each online community develops its own standards and rules about "normal" and "deviant" behavior, the Internet may also be promoting the diversification of cultural traditions.

Activity 8.3 Cultural traditions

1. What cultural traditions have you inherited? What do you think overlaps with your parents' generation? What so you think is "new" for your generation? What do you imagine that you will pass on to the next generation?

8-2-3 School

In our society, schools play a key role in educating people. But, because it is impossible to teach everything at school due to the limited time, any school curriculum has to be selective and cover only a limited number of topics. This leads to a discussion about what subjects to teach.

Which subjects are more important than others? Are English and Mathematics more important than Biology and Art History? Also, who decides this? Who decides what subjects are more important? Should schools avoid teaching about controversial issues such as date rape, designer babies, and war atrocities? Should they teach controversial issues in a balanced way so that students can judge for themselves?

In this way, critical thinking is an important part of any education. However, if schools teach controversial issues, teachers need to give equal weight to all points of view about it, even if the evidence strongly suggests that one side is wrong. In this sense, what is taught may not be as important as the way it is taught.

Activity 8.4 School curricula

1. What controversial issues do you recall learning about at school? How were they taught?

2. If you don't recall learning about controversial issues, do you think you should have?

3. Design a lesson plan for teaching junior high school students about a controversial issue that you are interested in.

8-2-4 The news media

The news media strongly influence our picture of the world. Especially, if you are studying International Relations, you ca get a lot of information from the news media, including BBC, Al Jazeera, CNN and so on. We can access many kinds of information thanks to freedom of speech. However, does freedom of speech really mean that we can say anything we want to? Likewise, can the media say anything it wants to? The media, like us, has to be responsible in what it says.

But, there is another important point here. Even if the media is responsible in what is says, it can still choose what it wants to say and what it doesn't want to say. In this way, the media can select what news it wants to tell, and how to tell that news. In other words, there are always biases in the news media.

The first bias is what we call *agenda setting*. In a meeting, the agenda is the list of topics that will be discussed. If something is not on the agenda, it generally doesn't get discussed. So, for a particular news media, the agenda is the news that they want the public to discuss. What they don't cover, the public can't discuss. This means that the news media can influence public debates by deciding what is news and what is not. If you compare different newspapers, you may notice that different papers cover different topics. They also cover stories in different degrees of detail. This is because they select the stories they want to tell.

The second bias is called *framing bias*. This concerns how a news story is presented. How a news story is framed will influence how it is discussed. For example, even though different newspapers cover the same topic, their story could be totally different! This is because they want to frame the story in a certain way. The news story will be framed, or told, from their perspective.

Activity 8.5 Comparing media agendas and frames

1. *Make a list of the topics on page one for at least two or three different newspapers covering a one-week period (Don't use FB or Line news: they are chosen according to your online personality.) Try some combination of the paper versions of (1) the mainstream daily papers {Yomiuri, Mainichi, Asahi}, compared with some (2) less mainstream papers {Seikyo, Akahata, Kyoto, Ryukyu Shinpo, Okinawa Times, etc.}.*

   How many topics overlap? How many do not? What can we suggest in terms of agenda-setting?

2. *What can be said about the way in which different newspapers frame different stories?*

   Obtain an editorial from one of the mainstream newspapers listed above concerning US military bases in Japan, and compare it with an equivalent editorial from one of the Okinawan newspapers on the same topic.

8-2-5 Expert opinion

How far is the Sun from the Earth? How will international relations change after the UK exit from the European Union? These questions are not easy to answer. We often need expert opinion to explain complex things and help us to understand them. Experts have studied their field for a long time. They have read and written a lot about their area of expertise. They have discussed their topic with other experts. Because of this, we can trust the opinions of experts regarding their field. But, we need to be careful. Experts, just like everybody else, sometimes make mistakes. It may also be that experts have their own biases. It is very difficult for us to predict the future. This is the same for experts. Even though, they may be able to make educated guesses about what could happen in the future, they often get it wrong. For example, not many experts predicted the end of the Cold War. Almost no one predicted the historic victory of Donald Trump in the 2016 US presidential elections.

8-3 Why is personal knowledge important?

As mentioned previously, much of our personal knowledge actually comes from second-hand sources, especially the Internet or news media. Because of this, some people say that the important thing is to know where to find the information you need. But, what if the information you find on the Internet is not true? Or what if such information is heavily biased? How can you trust such sources? It is here that personal knowledge plays a key role in critical thinking. Critical thinking is the ability to think clearly and rationally about what to do or what to believe. It is your ability to think independently. To be a good critical thinker, a good memory or knowing a lot of facts is not enough. Rather, you need to know how to make use of such knowledge to solve problems. In this way, students should not just 'repeat' or 'remember' what you are being taught. Students need to 'doubt' first, and then think logically and deeply. Students must 'ponder' the information, which means to take time to slowly and carefully consider it.

8-3-1 The Internet and critical thinking

It often seems that the Internet lets you get anything you want. You can get information about news, gossip, and even recipes for dinner. If you want to get information about a country that you planning to visit, you can simply go online to check things out. If you want to learn how to do something like fix your bicycle brakes or change a watch battery, there are a lot of free videos available online. You can find a wide variety of information very quickly, and you can know what is happening in the world in real time. In this Internet age, knowing where to find answers you can trust is very important.

Some people worry that the Internet is killing people's critical thinking ability. Firstly, because the Internet gives us so much information, only knowing a little about many things may satisfy people. People may think they don't need to understand why events happen. In this way, we could say that quantity is more important that quality. It may be that many people are happy to get the answers they seek quickly. Such people are not interested in thinking deeply.

Secondly, people tend to only read news stories, or collect information that is interesting for them. Indeed, we can now set "our news" on news websites. With these settings we can see only news that we are interested in. SNS services also have complex logarithms that choose what to show us. These algorithms were designed for targeted advertising, but are also used for news stories. This means that the information we are shown is the information we prefer. Our preferences are deciding which information we receive. We do this consciously too. For example, if you believe in UFOs, then you will likely only look for information that proves their existence. You would likely ignore the evidence that proves the opposite. If we continue to get information only in this way, we will fall into the trap of confirmation bias. In other words, we only collect information that supports what we believe, and tend to ignore any counter-evidence.

Activity 8.6 Examining Internet trends

Examine Google's big data on recent Internet search trends:

https://www.google.com/trends/hottrends

What does the data suggest about the most common reasons people use the Internet?

Take a vague belief that you have, and see if you can find support for it online.

Third, there is no quality control on the Internet. You can find almost limitless information on the Internet, but how can you tell what is the truth? Because of technological improvements, people from all over the world have access to computers at school and Internet cafes, and anyone can access the Internet even from the most remote place on the planet by using a Smartphone to upload their own contents. Almost anyone can become the source of information on the Internet.

If we consider all of these issues, we can see that critical thinking is necessary for us. If we cannot think critically, we could believe untrue things, and we could support and follow people whose ideas are unsafe. This is why personal knowledge is crucial.

8-4 Obstacles to personal knowledge

Obviously, to be a good critical thinker, you need to be well informed. You need to have enough safe information to be able make knowledge that can be used as the base for decisions and action. However, people tend to mix up their own beliefs and opinions with genuine knowledge. This tendency reduces our ability to think critically. Generally speaking, one or more of the following five obstacles to personal knowledge causes this.

8-4-1 Ignorance

We are not superhuman and it is natural that we do not know everything about the world. If we do not know something, we can simply go and find the answer. However, there is a real risk of us being overconfident and believing we know more than we actually know. It seems that many humans have a strong tendency to do this, as seen in our tendency to make hasty generalizations. It means that we think we understand something, when in fact we don't.

This is the problem of ignorance in our personal knowledge. It is sometimes called 'our ignorance of our ignorance', because we do not know that we are ignorant. Or to put it another way, we do not know that we do not know. For example, if you are asked a trivial question such as 'Is New York north or south of Rome?' You may answer that New York is north of Rome. Perhaps we feel justified in making this response because we have an image of Rome as sunny, and an image of New York having snowy winters. But in fact, it is slightly south of Rome. How about this question: 'In which city was the United Nations Charter, that created the United Nations, signed by its founding members?' Perhaps many of you may choose New York, where the UN is headquartered, but it was in fact San Francisco!

Similarly, when you study abroad and are having a chat with your classmates about the country you are from, you may think you know everything about Japan. You may think that you have deep knowledge about Japan because you are Japanese. You may think you know about the economy, politics and culture of Japan. But, when someone asks you to explain about these topics, you might notice that you actually don't know as much as you thought you did. You may realize that your knowledge of Japan is in fact superficial, or thin. A similar thing may happen in an exam when you start thinking, "oh, I thought I knew this, but I can't explain it"! Indeed, in this way, being able to explain something to someone else is an indicator of knowledge. This is the reason why you have to write essays. We could say that writing an essay is really the only way to show that you have knowledge of something.

8-4-2 Apathy

We are basically self-interested beings. When we have a strong opinion about something, we do not easily change our minds. This is the problem of apathy in our personal knowledge. In other words, we only want to accept knowledge that fits with our interests, and we tend to ignore something that is difficult to understand. A common word that we could use here is "lazy". We often have lazy brains, meaning that we can't be bothered to challenge ourselves. For example, if I believe that God exists, I would not listen to people who oppose my belief because their ideas do not fit my belief.

Another related point is that, if we feel we do not know things compared to others, we may suddenly lose interest in that topic because we do not want to appear to know less. In these cases, we give up. Of course, it is perhaps best to study together, so that it is more interesting, and our motivation is higher. The danger with apathy is that there is no progress, no self-improvement, and no personal development. It would certainly be very strange for students to have apathy towards their studies. Apathy only leads towards narrow-mindedness, and this is the opposite of knowledge. Any knowledge, any opinion, any argument can only be improved by being challenged from different viewpoints.

8-4-3 Fantasy

We often think something is true because we want to believe it is true. However, if we keep telling ourselves that something is true simply because we want it to be true, it will cloud our minds. This is the problem of fantasy that can affect our personal knowledge. For example, many people believe 'what my government tells me is always right'. In Japan, many people believed nuclear power generation to be a clean, stable and cheap energy source because the government told them so. But now, many people clearly oppose nuclear power generation in Japan. This is basically due to the Fukushima Daiichi nuclear power disaster that happened on the 11th of March 2011. Even though the government has tried to tell people in Japan that nuclear power is safe, citizens do not believe it. Indeed, perhaps the real problem is not nuclear energy so much as trust in government.

8-4-4 Bias

Since our ways of thinking are influenced by many things, including personal character, the community that you were raised in, gender and sexual orientation, educational background, economic status, nationality and so on, everyone sees things from their own perspective. Our perspectives are subjective, or different for different people. In other words, it is very difficult to see things purely objectively.

Subjectivity is not necessarily a bad thing. Together, humans are able to cooperate, collaborate and innovate. Different perspectives make this possible. Furthermore, it would be very strange to have a society where everyone thinks totally the same way about everything, although this was a common fantasy in 20th century totalitarian fascism.

However, if our own ways of thinking are too narrow, and if we think that other ideas are strange and unacceptable, then we may end up with the problem of bias in our personal knowledge. If you think all people from a certain country are very rude and threatening to our peaceful life, then you will never get to know the good side of those people. Indeed, bias has a strong relationship with prejudice, which involves unfavorable opinions or feelings based on limited evidence.

8-4-5 Peer pressure

We all care about what others think of us. As long as we live in society, what others think of us will always be important. Although many of us have different ideas and views, we must all live together. That means we must adjust our beliefs to social norms. For example, because you do not feel that cold in December you want to wear short sleeves. But, it's likely that all your friends will wear long sleeves, and you don't want to appear strange. Likewise, in class, even though you know the answer to the teacher's question, you don't answer because you don't want other students to think you are "showing off". In this way peer pressure can be an obstacle to knowledge, because we just follow others. If our own way of thinking is strongly affected by others in this way, then our personal knowledge is negatively affected by peer pressure.

8-5 How to make objective judgments

So, even with all of these obstacles to personal knowledge, how can we make objective judgments? How can we build safe personal knowledge? We have looked at various obstacles to personal knowledge. Perhaps the best way to make our judgments objective is to always subject our own ideas to the critical scrutiny of other people.

This means, we should not think our own opinions are the only truth in the world. This will lead to overconfidence, which will result in mistakes, and believing in things that are not actually true. It is especially important for students not to fall into the apathy trap, and become uninterested in other's opinions. We must also be careful not to believe in things that are just fantasy. While imagination is sometimes necessary for knowledge, fantasy is not a base for building knowledge. Whilst all people have biases, if we are aware of them, we can limit their negative effect on our knowledge. Too, peer-pressure will limit our ability to create knowledge. Rather than fall into these traps, you should always have an external check on your knowledge. This is why any research outcome made by an individual researcher has to be presented at recognized academic conferences, and their academic papers must be peer-reviewed by well-acknowledged reviewers before it is made publicly available. This shows that personal knowledge must be developed though good communications with other people. It requires open-minded yet critical thinking.

Finally, developing personal knowledge also requires some courage. That is, exposing your ideas and thinking to others so that they can be improved is a necessary and useful thing, but it may need some courage!

M.I.

The authors

Russell Garofalo, Masahiko Iguchi, Noah McCormack, Patrick Strefford all teach in the International Relations Department at Kyoto Sangyo University.

This publication does not differ in content from the book published by BookWay in 2017.
本書は 2017 年に BookWay より発行された書籍と内容に相違はありません。

On Knowledge and Learning
A concise introduction to the humanities

2024年 3 月25日　初版発行

著　者　Russell Garofalo, Masahiko Iguchi,
　　　　Noah McCormack, Patrick Strefford

発行所　学術研究出版（Academic Research Publication）
　　　　〒670-0933　兵庫県姫路市平野町62
　　　　［販売］Tel. 079(280)2727　Fax. 079(244)1482
　　　　［制作］Tel. 079(222)5372
　　　　https://arpub.jp

印刷所　小野高速印刷株式会社
©Noah McCormack, Patrick Strefford 2024,
Printed in Japan
ISBN978-4-911008-55-3